Enlarged Print Edition

Oxford Picture Dictionary of American English

Monolingual English Edition

E. C. PARNWELL

ILLUSTRATED BY
BERNARD CASE
CORINNE CLARKE
RAY BURROWS

OXFORD UNIVERSITY PRESS · 1984

Oxford University Press
200 Madison Avenue, New York, N.Y. 10016 USA

Walton Street Oxford OX2 6DP
OXFORD is a trademark of Oxford University Press

© Oxford University Press 1984

First edition published 1978

Library of Congress Cataloging in Publication Data

Parnwell, E. C.
Oxford picture dictionary of American English.
Includes index.
SUMMARY: Teaches English as a second language through the use of pictures
dealing with everyday topics such as the body, post office, law, travel, and
family.
1. English language in the United States.
2. Picture dictionaries, English. 3. English language—Text-books for
foreigners. [1. English language—Textbooks for foreigners] I. Case, Bernard.
II. Clarke, Corinne. III. Burrows, Ray. IV. Title.
PE2835.5.P3   423   77-18490   ISBN 0-19-502332-3

Note to the teacher

We are proud to present the first contextualized Oxford Picture Dictionary using
American English. This dictionary can be used for communicative purposes. It
will stimulate exciting conversations about everyday topics which students come
in contact with. It can also be used as a handy reference for students studying on
their own.

Printing (last digit): 9 8 7 6 5 4 3
Printed in Hong Kong

CONTENTS

4 Our Universe
5 The World
8 The Human Body
10 Clothes
14 In the City
16 The Law
17 Fire and Medical Services
18 Education
20 In the Supermarket
21 In the Office
22 At the Post Office
23 On a Building Site
24 In a Workshop
25 Tools
26 A House
27 The Weather/The Yard
28 The Hall
29 The Living Room
30 The Kitchen
31 Household Objects
32 The Bedroom/The Baby
33 The Bathroom
34 In the Country
35 Camping and the Seaside
36 On the Farm
37 Power
38 Travel
45 National Defense
46 Recreation
53 Sewing
54 Occupations/Professions
56 Animals
61 Plants
64 Verbs
67 Containers
68 Lines and Shapes
69 Measurement
70 Time, Date, Temperature
71 Family Relationships
72 Nouns of Quantity
74 Adjectives
76 Prepositions
78 Index

A.	**In Space**	B.	**Phases of the Moon**	C.	**Space Travel**
1.	comet	10.	eclipse	15.	nosecone
2.	constellation	11.	new/crescent	16.	rocket
3.	galaxy		moon	17.	launch(ing) pad
4.	planet	12.	half moon	18.	satellite
5.	star	13.	full moon	19.	(space) capsule
6.	Moon	14.	old moon	20.	astronaut
7.	Earth			21.	spacesuit
8.	Sun				
9.	orbit				

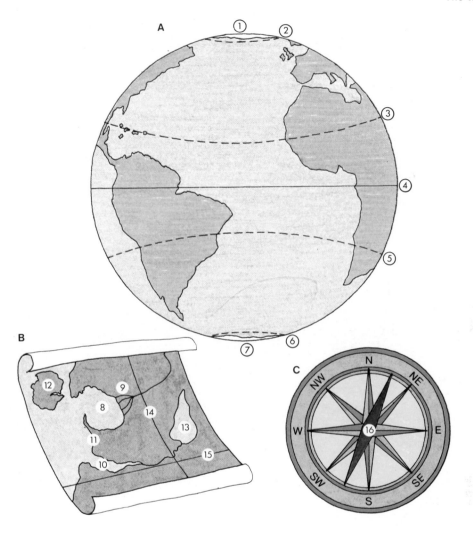

A. Globe
1. North Pole
2. Arctic Circle
3. Tropic of Cancer
4. Equator
5. Tropic of Capricorn
6. Antarctic Circle
7. South Pole

B. Map
8. bay
9. delta
10. estuary
11. coastline
12. island
13. lake
14. line of longitude
15. line of latitude

C. Compass
16.	needle
N	north
NE	northeast
E	east
SE	southeast
S	south
SW	southwest
W	west
NW	northwest

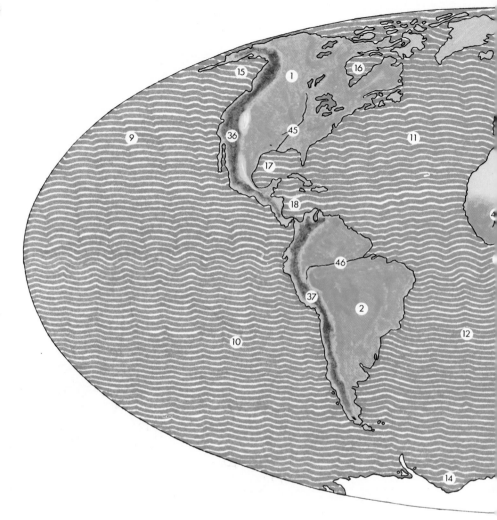

Continents
1. North America
2. South America
3. Europe
4. Africa
5. Asia
6. Australia
7. Antarctica

Oceans
8. Arctic
9. North Pacific
10. South Pacific

11. North Atlantic
12. South Atlantic
13. Indian
14. Southern

Seas, Gulfs, Bays
15. Gulf of Alaska
16. Hudson Bay
17. Gulf of Mexico
18. Caribbean Sea
19. Gulf of Guinea
20. North Sea
21. Baltic Sea

22. Mediterranean Sea
23. Black Sea
24. Caspian Sea
25. Red Sea
26. Persian Gulf
27. Arabian Sea
28. Bay of Bengal
29. Coral Sea
30. Tasman Sea
31. South China Sea
32. East China Sea
33. Sea of Japan
34. Sea of Okhotsk
35. Bering Sea

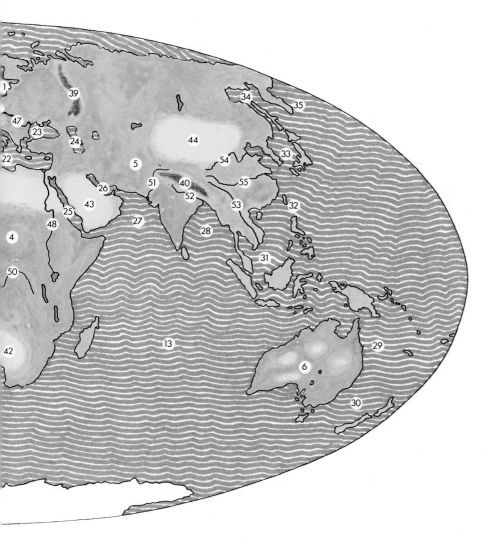

Mountain Ranges

36. Rockies
37. Andes
38. Alps
39. Urals
40. Himalayas

Deserts

41. Sahara
42. Kalahari
43. Arabian
44. Gobi

Rivers

45. Mississippi
46. Amazon
47. Danube
48. Nile
49. Niger
50. Congo
51. Indus
52. Ganges
53. Mekong
54. Yellow
55. Yangtze

A

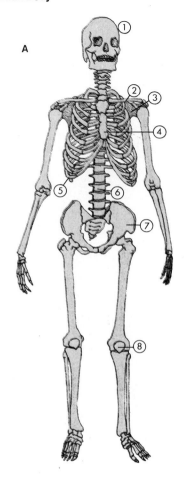

B

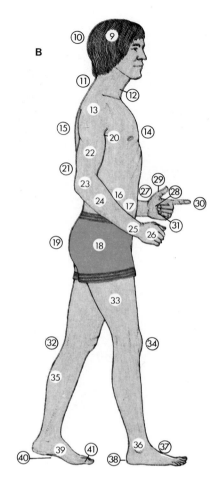

A.	**The Skeleton**	13.	shoulder	28.	palm
1.	skull	14.	chest	29.	thumb
2.	collar bone	15.	back	30.	finger
3.	shoulder blade	16.	waist	31.	nail/fingernail
4.	breastbone	17.	stomach/abdomen	32.	leg
5.	rib	18.	hip	33.	thigh
6.	backbone/spine	19.	buttocks	34.	knee
7.	hip bone/pelvis	20.	armpit	35.	calf
8.	kneecap	21.	arm	36.	ankle
		22.	upper arm	37.	foot
B.	**The Body**	23.	elbow	38.	heel
9.	hair	24.	forearm	39.	instep
10.	head	25.	wrist	40.	sole
11.	neck	26.	fist	41.	toe
12.	throat	27.	hand		

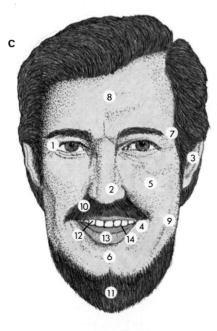

C

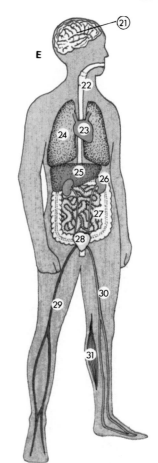

E

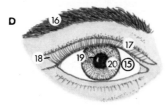

D

C. The Face

1. eye
2. nose
3. ear
4. mouth
5. cheek
6. chin
7. temple
8. forehead
9. jaw
10. mustache
11. beard
12. tooth
13. lip
14. tongue

D. The Eye

15. eyeball
16. eyebrow
17. eyelid
18. eyelashes
19. pupil
20. iris

E. The Insides

21. brain
22. windpipe
23. heart
24. lung
25. liver
26. kidney
27. intestines
28. bladder
29. vein
30. artery
31. muscle

1.	bathrobe	9.	(cardigan) sweater
2.	pajamas	10.	loafer
3.	slipper	11.	shoe
4.	undershirt/T-shirt	12.	rubber boot
5.	(under)shorts	13.	sneaker/tennis shoe
6.	sock	14.	jeans
7.	jacket/sport coat	15.	sweater
8.	slacks	16.	belt
		17.	buckle
		18.	boot
		19.	jacket

1. shirt	13. hat	25. cuff links
2. collar	14. overcoat/coat	26. button
3. cuff	15. lapel	27. jacket/sport coat
4. tie	16. pocket	28. briefcase/attaché
5. vest	17. trousers/pants/	case
6. suit	slacks	29. slacks
7. sleeve	18. cuff	30. rain hat
8. shoe	19. scarf	
9. shoelace	20. glove	
10. sole	21. watch	
11. heel	22. watchband	
12. trenchcoat/	23. glasses	
raincoat	24. umbrella	

1. bra	9. earring	17. face cream
2. slip	10. necklace	18. lipstick
3. panties	11. nail file	19. comb
4. panty hose	12. compact	20. brush
5. nightgown	13. mascara	21. bathrobe
6. slipper	14. nail polish	22. roller
7. ring	15. perfume	23. clip
8. bracelet	16. eye shadow	

1. turtleneck sweater	7. (suit)jacket	13. barrette
2. pantsuit	8. skirt	14. jeans
3. boot	9. handkerchief	15. shirt
4. (shoulder) bag/ purse	10. dress	16. sweater
5. suit	11. coat	17. sandal
6. blouse	12. (knee)sock	

1. mailbox
2. crosswalk
3. subway station
4. taxi/taxicab
5. bicycle
6. traffic light
7. street sign
8. curb
9. gutter
10. drain/sewer
11. park
12. bridge
13. van
14. truck
15. intersection
16. motorcycle

17.	baby carriage	22.	street light	27.	trash can/basket
18.	apartment house	23.	parking meter	28.	telephone booth
19.	office building	24.	bus	29.	parking lot
20.	store	25.	bus stop	30.	car
21.	display window	26.	sidewalk	31.	street/road

A.   Detection

1. policeman/police officer
2. gun
3. uniform
4. police station
5. police car
6. police dog
7. nightstick
8. handcuffs
9. flashlight
10. magnifying glass
11. fingerprints
12. footprints

B.   Jail

13. guard
14. prisoner
15. cell
16. bars

C.   Court of Law

17. jury
18. witness stand
19. witness
20. defendant/accused
21. defense attorney/lawyer
22. judge
23. prosecuting attorney/lawyer
24. gown/robe
25. stenographer

A. Fire Department
1. fireman/firefighter
2. firefighter's hat
3. (fire) hose
4. (fire) hydrant
5. fire extinguisher
6. (firefighter's) boot
7. fire engine
8. ladder
9. nozzle
10. bell
11. fire escape
12. fire
13. smoke

B. At the Dentist
14. dental assistant
15. dentist's chair
16. dentist
17. drill
18. lamp/light

C. A Hospital Ward
19. (hospital) bed
20. patient
21. doctor
22. stethoscope
23. sling
24. X-ray
25. nurse
26. crutches
27. bandage/cast

1. teacher
2. blackboard
3. eraser
4. chalk
5. student
6. book bag
7. desk
8. pencil
9. pen
10. ruler
11. compass
12. protractor
13. glue
14. book
15. notebook
16. slide rule
17. loose-leaf paper
18. loose-leaf notebook
19. map
20. calendar

1. scales	9. microscope	16. flask
2. pan	10. lens	17. crystals
3. weights	11. slide	18. pipette
4. meter	12. Bunsen burner	19. magnet
5. dial	13. tripod	20. pestle
6. needle/pointer	14. rubber tubing	21. mortar
7. bench	15. beaker	22. test tube
8. stool		

1. shopping cart	11. eggs	20. cookies
2. cashier	12. hot dogs	21. cake
3. cash register	13. meat	22. fish
4. checkout counter	14. freezer	23. receipt
5. customer	15. shelf	24. bills
6. sack/bag	16. canned food	25. coins
7. (shopping) basket	17. fruit	26. crackers
8. clerk	18. vegetables	27. potatoes
9. cheese	19. bread	28. soap powder/
10. milk		detergent

1. desk	10. bulletin board	19. file/filing cabinet
2. telephone	11. envelope	20. carbon paper
3. calculator	12. in-box	21. typewriter
4. blotter	13. wastepaper basket	22. secretary
5. appointment book	14. photocopier	23. steno pad
6. hole puncher	15. switchboard	24. bookcase
7. stapler	16. operator	25. receptionist
8. adding machine	17. calendar	26. card file
9. paper clip	18. file	27. pencil holder

1. postal clerk	8. postmark	15. envelope
2. scale	9. stamp	16. flap
3. counter	10. (airmail) envelope	17. telegram/cable
4. mailbox	11. address	18. money order
5. mailman/mail carrier	12. return address	19. package
6. mailbag	13. zip code	20. string
7. aerogram	14. postcard	21. label

1. crane	9. drainpipe	17. trowel
2. bricklayer	10. foundations	18. hod
3. rafters	11. board	19. level
4. shingle	12. pick(ax)	20. excavator
5. ladder	13. shovel	21. cement mixer
6. rung	14. workman/worker	22. dump truck
7. scaffolding	15. sand	23. pneumatic drill
8. bricks	16. cement	24. wheelbarrow

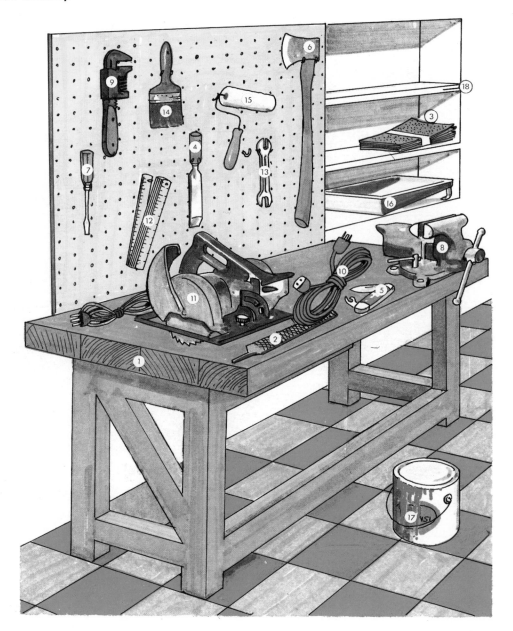

1. workbench	7. screwdriver	13. wrench
2. file	8. vise	14. paintbrush
3. sandpaper	9. monkey wrench	15. (paint) roller
4. chisel	10. extension cord	16. (paint) pan
5. pocket knife	11. power saw	17. paint can
6. axe	12. folding rule	18. shelf

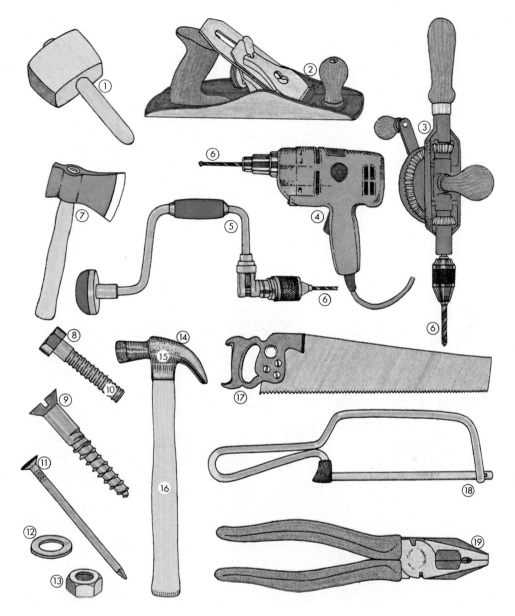

1. mallet	8. bolt	14. hammer
2. plane	9. screw	15. head
3. hand drill	10. thread	16. handle
4. electric drill	11. nail	17. saw
5. brace	12. washer	18. hacksaw
6. bit	13. nut	19. pliers
7. hatchet		

1. roof	8. window	15. blind
2. chimney	9. window frame	16. gutter
3. (outside) wall	10. windowpane	17. drainpipe
4. balcony	11. (window) sill	18. doormat
5. patio	12. shutter	19. antenna/aerial
6. garage	13. window box	20. (tool) shed
7. (front) door	14. curtain	21. grass

The Weather

1. lightning
2. (storm) cloud
3. rain
4. raindrops
5. snow
6. snowball
7. snowman
8. icicle
9. sun
10. sky

In the Yard

11. tree
12. trunk
13. branch
14. twigs
15. leaves
16. gate
17. hedge
18. path
19. lawn

20. flower
21. flower bed
22. bush
23. watering can
24. flower pot
25. pitchfork
26. shed
27. wheelbarrow
28. clothesline
29. laundry
30. clothespin

1. door	9. (coat) rack	16. light
2. mail slot	10. hook	17. (light) switch
3. lock and chain	11. stair	18. telephone/phone
4. bolt	12. staircase	19. receiver
5. hinge	13. banister	20. dial
6. (door) mat	14. upstairs	21. cord
7. floor	15. downstairs	22. telephone book
8. rug		

1. ceiling	11. armchair	21. record
2. wall	12. newspaper	22. (record) jacket
3. carpet	13. chair	23. coffee table
4. fireplace	14. magazine rack	24. radio
5. mantel	15. magazine	25. end table
6. fire	16. bookcase	26. lamp
7. curtain	17. shelf	27. lampshade
8. drape	18. amplifier	28. television/TV
9. couch/sofa	19. turntable	29. ashtray
10. cushion	20. speaker	

1. stove	15. bread box	28. napkin
2. oven	16. shelf	29. napkin holder
3. broiler	17. (tea) kettle	30. place mat
4. burner	18. toaster	31. knife
5. refrigerator	19. electric can opener	32. spoon
6. cabinet	20. coffee pot	33. fork
7. sink	21. can opener	34. plate
8. counter	22. can	35. bowl
9. garbage can	23. bottle opener	36. glass
10. fruit basket	24. dishwasher	37. cup
11. fruit	25. dish towel	38. sugar bowl
12. pot	26. table	39. saltshaker
13. pan	27. chair	40. pepper shaker
14. skillet/frying pan		

1. vacuum cleaner	8. dustpan	15. plug
2. broom	9. scouring powder	16. outlet/socket
3. ironing board	10. scrub brush	17. switch
4. washing machine	11. iron	18. soap powder/
5. mop	12. cord	detergent
6. dust brush	13. (light) bulb	19. pail/bucket
7. dustcloth	14. hair dryer	

The Bedroom

1. bed
2. headboard
3. pillow
4. pillowcase
5. sheet
6. blanket
7. bedspread
8. mattress
9. night table
10. dressing table
11. dressing table skirt
12. stool
13. mirror

14. closet
15. desk
16. chest of drawers
17. rug
18. toy box
19. toy
20. game
21. hair brush
22. comb
23. box of tissues
24. jewelry box
25. alarm clock

The Baby

26. crib
27. sleeper
28. pacifier
29. stuffed animal
30. rattle
31. doll
32. changing table
33. bottle
34. nipple
35. bib
36. diaper
37. baby powder

1. bathtub/tub	12. sink	22. towel
2. hot water faucet	13. razor	23. towel rack
3. cold water faucet	14. (razor) blade	24. (bathroom) scale
4. shower head	15. shaving mug	25. bath mat
5. drain	16. shaving brush	26. sponge
6. drain plug	17. toothbrush	27. soap
7. diverter	18. glass	28. hamper
8. toilet	19. washcloth	29. tile
9. handle	20. nail brush	30. curtain rod
10. toilet paper	21. toothpaste	31. shower curtain
11. medicine chest		

1. plateau	8. woods/wood	14. hedge
2. mountain	9. forest	15. tree
3. (mountain) peak	10. hill	16. village
4. waterfall	11. meadow	17. (foot) path
5. lake	12. river	18. road
6. valley	13. field	19. pond
7. stream		

1. tent	14. (beach) towel	26. beach ball
2. groundcloth	15. mask/goggles	27. seashell
3. sleeping bag	16. snorkel	28. pebbles
4. backpack	17. ice cream	29. rocks
5. camp(ing) stove	18. windbreaker	30. kite
6. cliff	19. deck chair	31. water
7. hotel	20. bathing trunks	32. surf
8. cottage	21. flipper	33. wave
9. boardwalk	22. sand	34. motorboat
10. seawall	23. sandcastle	35. swimmer
11. beach	24. bucket/pail	36. bathing suit
12. beach umbrella	25. shovel	37. seaweed
13. sunbather		

1. hayloft	13. scarecrow	25. horse
2. hay	14. wheat	26. mane
3. cow shed	15. farmer	27. hoof
4. barn	16. combine	28. saddle
5. pen	17. irrigation canal	29. sheep
6. barnyard	18. tractor	30. lamb
7. farm house	19. plow	31. duckling
8. field	20. furrow	32. duck
9. pond	21. cow	33. hen/chicken
10. fence	22. calf	34. rooster
11. fruit tree	23. bull	35. chick
12. orchard	24. goats	

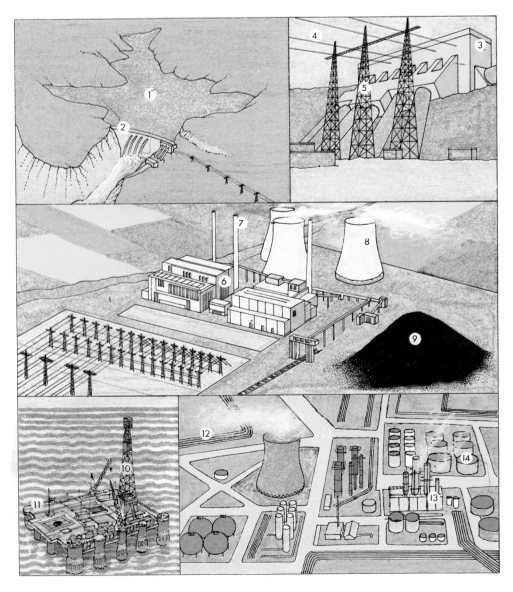

1. reservoir	6. power station	11. oil-rig
2. dam	7. smokestack	12. pipeline
3. powerhouse	8. cooling tower	13. refinery
4. cable	9. coal	14. storage tank
5. pylon	10. derrick	

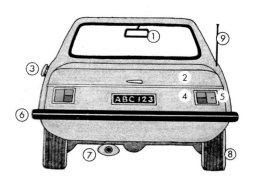

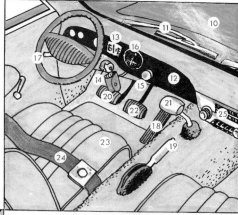

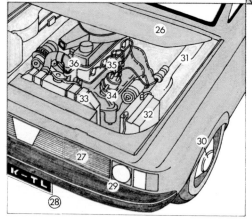

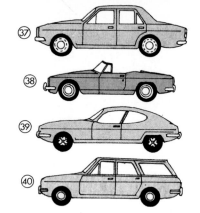

The Car

1. rearview mirror	14. ignition	27. grill
2. trunk	15. choke	28. license plate
3. gas cap	16. speedometer	29. headlight
4. taillight	17. steering wheel	30. hubcap
5. turn signal	18. accelerator	31. engine
6. bumper	19. hand/emergency	32. battery
7. exhaust (pipe)	brake	33. radiator
8. tire	20. clutch	34. distributor
9. antenna/aerial	21. gearshift	35. spark plug
10. windshield	22. brake	36. cylinder head
11. windshield wiper	23. seat	37. sedan
12. dashboard	24. seat/safety belt	38. convertible
13. fuel/gas gauge	25. car radio	39. sports coupe
	26. hood	40. station wagon

1.	thruway/highway/ freeway/ expressway	9.	air pump	16.	car
2.	overpass	10.	attendant	17.	bus
3.	underpass	11.	trailer truck/ tractor trailer	18.	sports car
4.	(traffic) circle	12.	transporter	19.	oil truck
5.	left/outside lane	13.	trailer	20.	motorcycle
6.	right/inside lane	14.	truck	21.	trailer
7.	gas station	15.	ambulance	22.	van
8.	gas pump				

1. bicycle/bike	14. brake	27. crash helmet
2. bell	15. crossbar	28. goggles
3. mirror	16. pump	29. motor scooter
4. cable	17. pedal	30. rear light
5. headlight	18. chain	31. seat
6. handlebars	19. sprocket	32. accelerator
7. seat	20. reflector	33. brake
8. saddlebag	21. taxi stand	34. saddlebag
9. wheel	22. taxi(cab)/cab	35. exhaust (pipe)
10. mudguard	23. meter	36. starter
11. tire	24. fare	37. footrest
12. spokes	25. (taxi) driver	38. gearshift
13. valve	26. passenger	

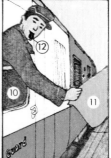

1. train	11. flag	21. platform number
2. engineer	12. whistle	22. signalman
3. engine	13. (train) station	23. signal box
4. coach/car	14. ticket office	24. (railroad) track
5. compartment	15. schedule	25. (railroad) ties
6. conductor	16. gateman	26. (railroad) switch
7. ticket	17. gate	27. signals
8. seat	18. waiting room	28. freight car
9. luggage rack	19. passengers	29. buffer/bumper
10. brakeman	20. platform	30. siding

1. horizon	7. ship	13. buoy
2. pier	8. hold	14. bollard
3. warehouse	9. smokestack	15. cable
4. crane	10. gangway	16. windlass
5. wharf	11. anchor	17. forklift
6. cargo	12. dock	

1. sailboat	8. oarlock	15. ferry
2. sail	9. canoe	16. barge
3. mast	10. paddle	17. trawler
4. rudder	11. motorboat	18. tanker
5. keel	12. outboard motor	19. deck
6. rowboat	13. bow	20. ocean liner
7. oar	14. stern	21. smokestack

1. customs	8. steward/flight attendant	15. helicopter
2. customs officer	9. (air)plane/airliner	16. rotor
3. passport	10. fuselage	17. light aircraft
4. luggage/baggage	11. wing	18. propeller
5. captain/pilot	12. jet engine	19. runway
6. passenger	13. tail/tail fin	20. control tower
7. stewardess/flight attendant	14. glider	21. hangar

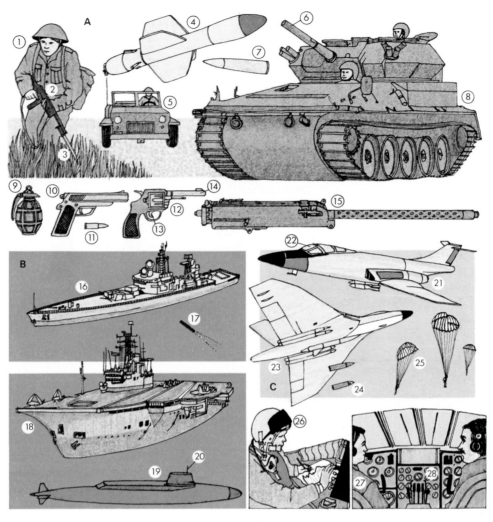

A. Army	12. revolver	**C. Air Force**
1. soldier	13. trigger	21. fighter plane
2. rifle	14. barrel	22. cockpit
3. bayonet	15. machine gun	23. bomber
4. guided missile		24. bomb
5. jeep	**B. Navy**	25. parachute
6. gun	16. warship	26. navigator
7. shell	17. torpedo	27. pilot
8. tank	18. aircraft carrier	28. control panel
9. (hand) grenade	19. submarine	
10. pistol	20. periscope	
11. bullet/cartridge		

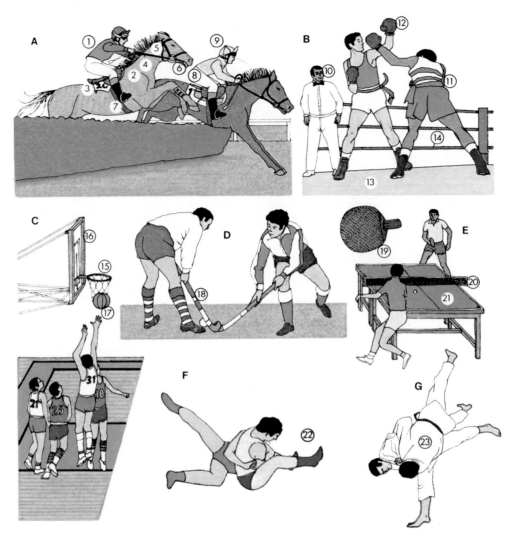

A. (Horse) Racing
1. jockey
2. (race)horse
3. saddle
4. reins
5. bridle
6. bit
7. stirrup
8. jodhpurs
9. cap

B. Boxing
10. referee
11. boxer
12. (boxing) glove
13. ring
14. ropes

C. Basketball
15. basket
16. backboard
17. ball

D. Field Hockey
18. stick

E. Ping-Pong/Table Tennis
19. racket
20. net
21. table

F. Wrestling
22. wrestlers

G. Judo
23. judo suit

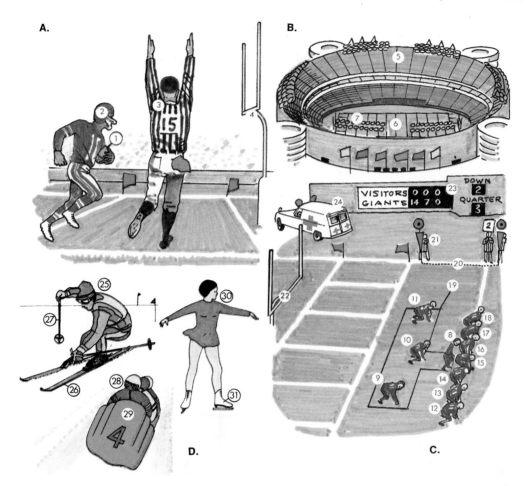

A. Football	**C. Line-Up**	20. chain
1. football	8. quarterback	21. linesman
2. helmet	9. right halfback	22. goalpost
3. referee	10. fullback	23. scoreboard
4. goalpost	11. left halfback	24. ambulance
	12. right end	
B. Stadium	13. right tackle	**D. Winter Sports**
5. (grand)stand	14. right guard	25. skier
6. field	15. center	26. ski
7. lights	16. left guard	27. (ski) pole
	17. left tackle	28. tobogganist
	18. left end	29. toboggan
	19. T formation	30. (ice)skater
		31. (ice)skate

Baseball
1. bat
2. batter
3. umpire
4. home plate
5. catcher
6. catcher's mask
7. mitt/glove
8. pitcher
9. first base
10. first baseman
11. second baseman
12. shortstop
13. third baseman
14. foul line
15. left fielder
16. center fielder
17. right fielder

Fishing
18. fisherman
19. (fishing) rod
20. line
21. hook
22. bait

Tennis
23. (tennis) court
24. net
25. server
26. service line
27. (tennis) racket
28. (tennis) ball

Orchestra
1. clarinet
2. valve
3. musician/player
4. violin
5. strings
6. bow
7. viola
8. cello
9. double bass
10. conductor
11. baton
12. (sheet) music
13. rostrum
14. horn
15. piano
16. keys
17. pedal
18. stool
19. trumpet
20. trombone
21. slide
22. saxophone
23. mouthpiece

Pop Group
24. singer
25. microphone
26. (electric) guitar
27. amplifier
28. (loud)speaker
29. cymbals
30. drum

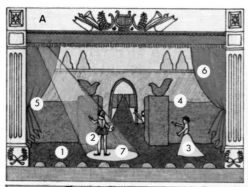
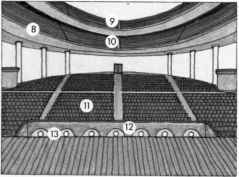
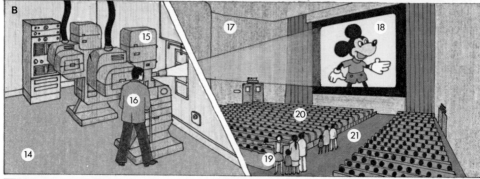

A. The Theater	10. balcony	18. screen
1. stage	11. orchestra	19. usherette/usher
2. actor	12. (orchestra) pit	20. seats
3. actress	13. footlights	21. aisle
4. set		
5. wings	**B. The Movies**	**C. The Library**
6. curtain	14. projection room	22. librarian
7. spotlight	15. projector	23. card catalog
8. theater	16. projectionist	24. desk
9. gallery	17. movie theater	25. bookshelf

1. (beer) bottle	13. soft drink	24. menu
2. bottle top	14. lighter	25. bottle of wine
3. stein/mug	15. bar	26. cork
4. (beer) can	16. draft beer	27. (wine) glass
5. matchbook	17. hard liquor	28. saltshaker
6. match	(scotch, gin, etc.)	29. pepper mill
7. bottle opener	18. cocktail waitress	30. pepper shaker
8. cigarette	19. bartender	31. tablecloth
9. ash	20. tap	32. napkin
10. ashtray	21. (bar)stool	33. check
11. corkscrew	22. waiter	34. jigger
12. straw	23. customer	

A. **Chess and Checkers**
1. chess set
2. board
3. pawn
4. rook/castle
5. knight
6. bishop
7. queen
8. king
9. checkers

B. **Cards**
10. (deck of) cards
11. jack of clubs

12. queen of diamonds
13. king of hearts
14. ace of spades

C. **Reading**
15. book
16. cover
17. (dust) jacket
18. spine
19. page
20. illustration
21. text

D. **Photography**
22. photograph/photo
23. negative
24. (roll of) film
25. camera
26. lens
27. screen
28. stand
29. (slide) projector
30. slide

1. sewing machine	11. pleat	19. wool
2. tape/seam binding	12. (common)/	20. pattern
3. seam	(straight) pin	21. knitting
4. hem	13. material/cloth	22. zipper
5. thimble	14. ruffle	23. hook and eye
6. needle	15. button	24. ribbon
7. elastic	16. buttonhole	25. tape measure
8. (spool of) thread	17. stitch	26. scissors
9. lace	18. knitting needle	27. snap
10. safety pin		

1. hairdresser
2. butcher
3. carpenter
4. bank teller
5. mechanic
6. longshoreman
7. miner
8. artist
9. typist
10. dressmaker/ seamstress
11. waitress
12. truck driver
13. clown
14. redcap/bellhop/ porter
15. announcer

1. fruit seller
2. electrician
3. gardener
4. photographer
5. florist
6. barber
7. baker
8. doctor
9. salesman/ salesperson
10. nurse
11. teacher
12. soldier
13. policeman/police officer
14. optician
15. sailor

1. horse	10. donkey	19. squirrel
2. foal	11. reindeer	20. rabbit
3. pig	12. antler	21. whisker
4. snout	13. dog	22. rat
5. llama	14. puppy	23. tail
6. camel	15. cat	24. fox
7. hump	16. kitten	25. bat
8. buffalo	17. paw	26. hedgehog
9. horn	18. mouse	

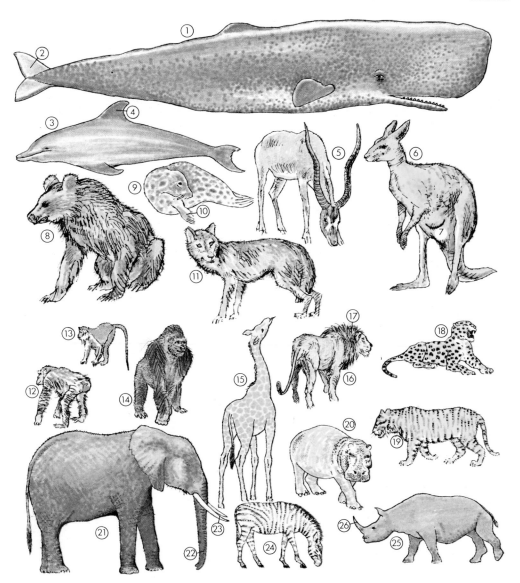

1. whale	10. flipper	19. tiger
2. tail/fluke	11. wolf	20. hippopotamus
3. dolphin	12. baboon	21. elephant
4. fin	13. monkey	22. trunk
5. antelope	14. gorilla	23. tusk
6. kangaroo	15. giraffe	24. zebra
7. pouch	16. lion	25. rhinoceros
8. bear	17. mane	26. horn
9. seal	18. leopard	

Fish and Other Animals

1. shark	10. eel	19. slug
2. fin	11. jellyfish	20. frog
3. swordfish	12. lobster	21. worm
4. salmon	13. snail	22. centipede
5. gill	14. shell	23. octopus
6. herring	15. sunfish	24. tentacle
7. tail	16. oyster	25. spider
8. snout	17. crab	26. (spider) web
9. scales	18. pincer/claw	27. scorpion

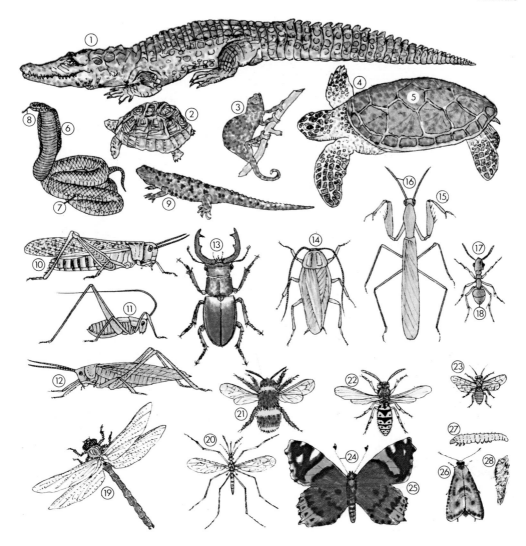

Reptiles
1. crocodile
2. tortoise
3. chameleon
4. turtle
5. shell
6. snake
7. scale
8. tongue
9. lizard

Insects
10. locust
11. cricket
12. grasshopper
13. beetle
14. cockroach
15. mantis
16. feeler
17. ant
18. abdomen

19. dragonfly
20. mosquito
21. bee
22. wasp
23. fly
24. antenna
25. butterfly
26. moth
27. caterpillar
28. cocoon

Birds

1. ostrich
2. eagle
3. claw
4. beak
5. feathers
6. hawk
7. owl
8. flamingo
9. webbed foot
10. vulture
11. peacock
12. crest
13. penguin
14. pheasant
15. heron
16. turkey
17. swan
18. canary
19. bill
20. parrot
21. (sea)gull
22. swallow
23. wing
24. dove
25. goose
26. parakeet
27. hummingbird
28. sparrow
29. nest
30. kingfisher
31. pigeon
32. blackbird
33. crow

Fruit

1. apple
2. stalk
3. skin
4. core
5. banana
6. peel
7. cherry
8. pit/stone
9. coconut
10. date
11. peanut
12. grapes
13. vine
14. lemon
15. mango
16. orange
17. sections
18. peel/rind
19. peach
20. pit/pip/stone
21. strawberry
22. pear
23. plum
24. pineapple
25. papaya
26. lichee
27. walnut
28. nutmeat
29. fig
30. grapefruit
31. cactus
32. fern
33. frond

Vegetables
1.   bean
2.   stalk
3.   pea
4.   pod
5.   carrot
6.   potato
7.   squash
8.   cucumber
9.   beet
10.   cauliflower

11.   cabbage
12.   lettuce
13.   onion
14.   mushroom
15.   tomato
16.   eggplant

Flowers
17.   daffodil
18.   daisy

19.   rose
20.   petal
21.   orchid
22.   tulip
23.   stem
24.   hibiscus
25.   bud
26.   waterlily
27.   sunflower
28.   seeds

1. (ear of) corn	9. sugar cane	17. bark
2. wheat	10. oak tree	18. log
3. olive	11. roots	19. palm
4. cocoa bean	12. trunk	20. fir
5. coffee berry	13. branch/bough	21. (pine)cone
6. cotton	14. twig	22. (pine) needles
7. rice	15. leaf	23. cedar
8. tea	16. acorn	24. willow

1. blow	10. dig	18. fall
2. break	11. dive	19. fight
3. carry	12. draw	20. fly
4. catch	13. drink	21. jump/leap
5. climb	14. dream	22. kick
6. crawl	15. drive	23. kneel
7. cry/weep	16. drown	24. laugh
8. cut	17. eat	25. lick
9. dance		

1. listen
2. open
3. lie
4. paint
5. pull
6. push
7. read
8. ride
9. run
10. sail
11. sew
12. shoot
13. shut
14. sing
15. sit
16. smile
17. stand
18. stir
19. sweep
20. swim
21. tear
22. touch
23. tie
24. walk
25. wash

1. wave	9. throw	17. clap
2. write	10. turn	18. iron
3. wind	11. give	19. sleep
4. bend	12. comb	20. hold
5. hit/beat	13. pass	21. type
6. hug	14. frown	22. boil
7. kiss	15. put	23. chop
8. pick	16. spin	

1. carton	9. thermos	15. box
2. paper bag/sack	10. plastic wrap	16. trunk
3. plastic garden bag/ trash bag	11. aluminum foil	17. crate
4. sandwich bag	12. trash can/garbage can	18. shopping bag
5. bottle	13. barrel	19. suitcase
6. jar	14. basket	20. carry-on case
7. can		21. wallet
8. paper cup		

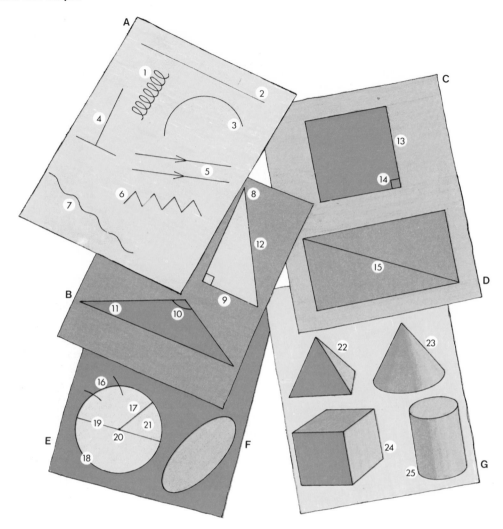

A.   Lines
1. spiral
2. straight line
3. curve
4. perpendicular line
5. parallel lines
6. zigzag
7. wavy line

B.   Triangles
8. apex
9. base
10. obtuse angle

11. acute angle
12. hypotenuse

C.   Square
13. side
14. right angle

D.   Rectangle/Oblong
15. diagonal

E.   Circle
16. arc
17. radius

18. circumference
19. diameter
20. center
21. section

F.   Oval/Ellipse

G.   Solid Figures
22. pyramid
23. cone
24. cube
25. cylinder

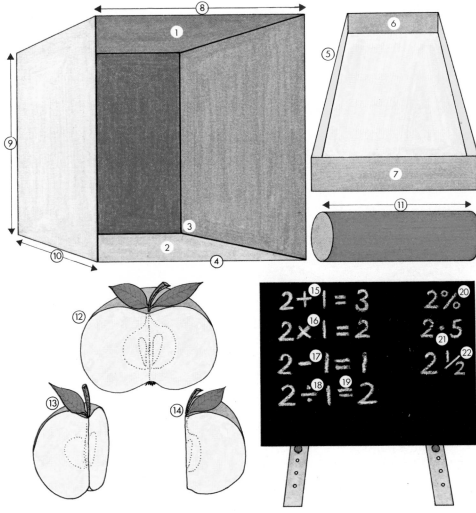

1. top
2. bottom
3. corner
4. edge
5. side
6. back
7. front
8. width
9. height
10. depth
11. length
12. a half
13. a third
14. a quarter
15. plus
16. multiplied by
17. minus
18. divided by
19. equals
20. per cent
21. decimal point
22. fraction

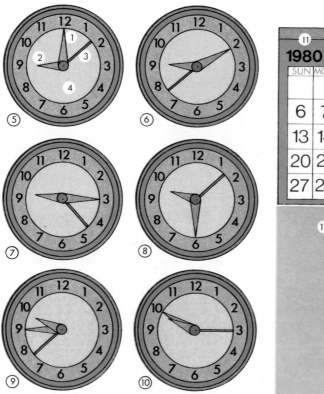

The Time
1. minute hand
2. hour hand
3. second hand
4. clock face
5. 9:00: nine o'clock
6. 9:10: ten after nine/ nine-ten
7. 9:15: a quarter after nine/nine-fifteen
8. 9:30: nine-thirty
9. 9:45: a quarter of ten/nine forty-five
10. 9:50: ten of ten/ nine-fifty

The Date
11. calendar
Today's date is Wednesday the sixteenth of July/July sixteenth nineteen eighty: July 16, 1980 or 7/16/80.

The Temperature
12. thermometer
The temperature is 18 degrees Centigrade (18° C) or 65 degrees Fahrenheit (65° F).

1. Alan and Ann are **husband** and **wife**.
2. Their **children** are Betty and Bob.
3. Their **daughter** is Betty and their **son** is Bob.
4. Alan is Bob's **father** and Ann is Bob's **mother**.
5. Betty is Bob's **sister** and Bob is Betty's **brother**.
6. Alan is Ben's **father-in-law** and Ann is his **mother in law**.
7. Ben is Alan and Ann's **son-in-law** and Brenda is their **daughter-in-law**.
8. Ben is Bob's **brother-in-law** and Brenda is Betty's **sister-in-law**.
9. Colin is Cliff and Carol's **cousin**.
10. Betty is Colin's **aunt** and Ben is his **uncle**.
11. Colin is Betty's **nephew** and Carol is Bob's **niece**.
12. Cliff is Ann and Alan's **grandson** and Carol is their **granddaughter**.

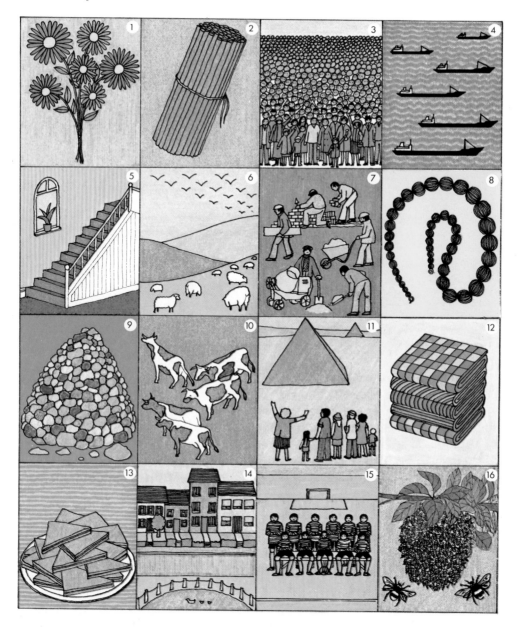

1. bunch (of flowers)
2. bundle (of sticks)
3. crowd (of people)
4. fleet (of ships)
5. flight (of stairs)
6. flock (of sheep or birds)
7. gang (of workmen/ workers)
8. string (of beads)
9. pile (of stones)
10. herd (of cattle)
11. group (of tourists)
12. pile (of blankets)
13. plate (of sandwiches)
14. row (of houses)
15. team (of players)
16. swarm (of bees)

1. ball (of string/
    twine)
2. box (of cookies)
3. bar (of soap)
4. glass (of milk)
5. bottle (of wine)
6. loaf (of bread)

7. lump (of sugar)
8. piece (of cake)
9. spool (of thread)
10. box (of matches)
    pack (of cigarettes)

11. cup (of coffee)
12. roll (of paper)
13. tube (of toothpaste)
14. bowl (of soup)

1. a) big/large
    b) little/small
2. a) blunt
    b) sharp
3. a) clean
    b) dirty
4. a) closed/shut
    b) open
5. a) crooked
    b) straight
6. a) shallow
    b) deep

7. a) wet
    b) dry
8. a) empty
    b) full
9. a) fast
    b) slow
10. a) fat
    b) thin
11. a) happy
    b) sad

12. a) easy
    b) difficult/hard
13. a) soft
    b) hard
14. a) high
    b) low
15. a) hot
    b) cold
16. a) long
    b) short

1. a) narrow
   b) wide
2. a) young
   b) old
3. a) new
   b) old
4. a) calm
   b) rough
5. a) rough
   b) smooth
6. a) strong
   b) weak

7. a) neat
   b) sloppy/messy
8. a) good
   b) bad
9. a) pretty/beautiful
   b) ugly
10. a) first
    b) last
11. a) light
    b) dark

12. a) light
    b) heavy
13. a) loud
    b) soft
14. a) solid
    b) hollow
15. a) thick
    b) thin
16. a) loose
    b) tight

1. **outside** the room	11. **out of** the drawer
2. **through** the door	12. **on** the table
3. **below** the picture	13. **on to/onto** the table
4. **down** the wall	14. **beside/next to** the
5. **up** the wall	table
6. **around** the neck	15. **by/near** the chair
7. **in front of** the chair	16. **behind** the chair
8. **against** the wall	17. **under/underneath/**
9. **into** the drawer	**beneath** the table
10. **in/inside** the	

1. **above** the trees
2. **beyond** the bridge
3. **from** the beach
4. **to** the beach
5. **among** the trees
6. **off** the road
7. **across/on** the road
8. **at** the corner
9. **along** the road
10. **toward** the bridge
11. **away from** the bridge
12. **between** the cars

The English Index includes a pronunciation guide and a phonemic transcription for each English word in the book.

There are two numbers after each word in the index. The first number refers to the page where the word is listed. The second number refers to the item number of the word.

For example: **abdomen** /ǽbdəmən/**59**/18 means that the word ''abdomen'' is the eighteenth item on page 59.

Vowels

/a/ as in calm /kam/	/ə/ as in butter /bə́tər/	/ɔ/ as in cough /kɔf/
/æ/ as in hat /hæt/	/i/ as in leak /lik/	/u/ as in broom /brum/
/e/ as in wait /wet/	/ɪ/ as in lick /lɪk/	/ʊ/ as in book /bʊk/
/ɛ/ as in wet /wɛt/	/o/ as in note /not/	

Consonants

/b/ as in base /bes/	/k/ as in cat /kæt/	/š/ as in ship /šɪp/
/č/ as in chip /čɪp/	/l/ as in lick /lɪk/	/t/ as in tin /tɪn/
/d/ as in dog /dɔg/	/m/ as in man /mæn/	/θ/ as in thin /θɪn/
/ð/ as in this /ðɪs/	/n/ as in win /wɪn/	/v/ as in vase /ves/
/f/ as in five /faɪv/	/ŋ/ as in sing /sɪŋ/	/w/ as in waist /west/
/g/ as in girl /gərl/	/p/ as in pin /pɪn/	/y/ as in yard / yard/
/h/ as in hand /hænd/	/r/ as in red /rɛd/	/z/ as in zebra /zíbrə/
/ǰ/ as in jacket /ǰǽkɪt/	/s/ as in sip /sɪp/	/ž/ as in measure /méžər/

/´/ over a vowel shows that the vowel has strong stress, eg. *address* /ǽdrɛs/ (noun), /ədrɛ́s/ (verb); *present* /prézɪnt/ (noun), /prɪzɛ́nt/ (verb).

INDEX

abdomen /ǽbdəmən/59/18; 8/17
above /əbʌ́v/77/1
accelerator /ɪkséləretər/38/18; 40/32
accused /əkyúzd/16/20
ace of spades /es-əv-spédz/52/14
acorn /ékɔrn/63/14
across /əkrɔ́s/77/7
actor /ǽktər/50/2
actress /ǽktrɪs/50/3
acute angle /əkyút-ǽŋgəl/68/11
adding machine /ǽdɪŋ-məšin/21/8
address /ədrés/22/11
adjective /ǽjɪktɪv/74–75
aerial /ǽriəl/26/19; 38/9
aerogram /ǽrogram/22/7
Africa /ǽfrɪkə/6/4
against /əgénst/76/8
air /ær/44
aircraft-carrier /ǽr-kræft-kæriər/45/18
Air-Force /ǽr-fɔrs/45
airplane /ǽr-plen/44/9
air-pump /ǽr-pəmp/39/9
airliner /ǽr-lainər/44/9
airmail envelope /ǽrmel-ɛnvəlop/22/10
airport /ǽr-pɔrt/44
aisle /ail/50/21
alarm-clock /əlárm-klak/32/25
along /əlɔ́ŋ/77/9
Alps /ǽlps/7/38
aluminum foil /əlúmɪnəm-fɔ́il/67/11
Amazon /ǽmazan/7/46
ambulance /ǽmbyuləns/39/15; 47/24
among /əmʌ́ŋ/77/5
amplifier /ǽmplɪfaiər/29/18; 49/27
anchor /ǽŋkər/42/11
Andes /ǽndiz/7/37
animal /ǽnəməl/56–60
ankle /ǽŋkəl/8/36
announcer /ənáunsər/54/15
ant /ænt/59/17
Antarctica /æntárktɪkə/6/7
Antarctic Circle /æntárktɪk-sárkəl/5/6
antelope /ǽtəlop/57/5
antenna /ænténə/26/19; 38/9
antler /ǽntlər/56/12
apartment house /əpártmənt-haus/15/18
apex /épɛks/68/8
apple /ǽpəl/61/1
appointment book /əpɔ́intmənt-buk/21/5
Arabian Desert /ərébiən-dézərt/7/43
Arabian Sea /ərébiən-sí/6/27
arc /ark/68/16
Arctic /árktɪk/6/8
Arctic Circle /arktɪk-sárkəl/5/2
arm /arm/8/21
armchair /árm-čɛr/29/11
armpit /ármpɪt/8/20
Army /ármi/45
around /əraúnd/76/6
artery /ártəri/9/30
artist /ártɪst/54/8
ash /æš/51/9
ashtray /ǽštre/29/29; 51/10
Asia /éžə/6/5
astronaut /ǽstrənɔt/4/20
at /æt/77/8
attache case /ætæšé-kes/11/28
attendant /əténdənt/39/10
aunt /ænt/71/10
Australia /ɔstrélyə/6/6
away from /əwé-frəm/77/11
axe /æks/24/6

baboon /bæbún/57/13
baby /bébi/32
baby carriage /bébi-kærij/15/17
babypowder /bébi-paudər/32/37
back /bæk/8/15; 69/6
backboard /bǽk-bɔrd/46/16
backbone /bǽk-bon/8/6
backpack /bǽk-pæk/35/4
bad /bæd/75/8
bag /bæg/13/4; 20/6
baggage /bǽgɪj/44/4
bait /bet/48/22

baker /békər/55/7
balcony /bǽlkəni/26/4; 50/10
ball /bɔl/46/17; 48/28; 73/1
ball of string /bɔ́l-əv-strɪ́ŋ/73/1
ball of twine /bɔ́l-əv-twáin/73/1
Baltic Sea /báltɪk-sí/6/21
banana /bənǽnə/61/5
bandage /bǽndɪj/17/27
banister /bǽnɪstər/28/13
bank teller /bǽŋk-telər/54/4
bar /bar/16/16; 51; 51/15; 73/2
barber /bárbər/55/6
barge /bárj/43/16
bark /bark/63/17
barn /barn/36/4
barnyard /barnyard/36/6
barrel /bǽrəl/45/14; 67/13
barrette /barét/13/13
barstool /bár-stul/51/21
bartender /bár-tendər/51/19
base /bes/68/9
baseball /bés-bɔl/48
basket /bǽskɪt/20/7; 46/15; 67/14
basketball /bǽskɪt-bɔl/46
bat /bæt/48/1; 56/25
bathmat /bǽθ-mæt/33/25
bathing suit /béðɪŋ-sut/35/36
bathing trunks /béðɪŋ-trəŋks/35/20
bathrobe /bæθ-rob/10/1; 12/21
bathroom /bǽθ-rum/33
bathroom scale /bǽθ-rum-skél/33/24
bath tub /bǽθ-təb/33/1
baton /bətán/49/11
batter /bǽtər/48/2
battery /bǽtəri/38/32
bay /be/5/8
Bay of Bengal /bé-av-bɛngɔ́l/6/28
bayonet /béyənɛt/45/3
beach /bič/35/11
beachball /bíčbɔl/35/26
beach towel /bíč-tauəl/35/14
beach umbrella /bíč-əmbrɛlə/35/12
beak /bik/60/4
beaker /bíkər/19/15
bean /bin/62/1
bear /bɛr/57/8
beard /bɪrd/9/11
beat /bit/66/5
beautiful /byútɪfəl/75/9a
bed /bed/32/1
bedroom /bédrum/32
bedspread /béd-spred/32/7
bee /bi/59/21
beer bottle /bír-batəl/51/1
beer can /bír-kæn/51/4
beet /bit/62/9
beetle /bítəl/59/13
behind /biháind/76/16
bell /bɛl/17/10; 40/2
bellhop /bélhap/54/14
below /biló/76/3
belt /belt/10/16
bench /bɛnč/19/7
bend /bend/66/4
beneath /biniθ/76/17
Bering Sea /bérɪŋ-sí/7/35
beside /bisáid/76/14
between /bitwín/77/12
beyond /biánd/77/2
bib /bɪb/32/35
bicycle /báisɪkəl/14/5; 40/1
big /bɪg/74/1a
bike /baik/40/1
bill /bɪl/60/19
bills /bɪlz/20/24
bird /bərd/60
bishop /bíšəp/52/6
bit /bɪt/25/6; 46/6
blackbird /blǽkbərd/60/32
blackboard /blǽkbɔrd/18/2
Black Sea /blǽk-sí/6/23
bladder /blǽdər/9/28
blade /bled/33/14
blanket /blǽŋkət/32/6
blind /blaind/26/15
blotter /blátər/21/4
blouse /blaus/13/6
blow /blo/64/1
blunt /blənt/74/2a

board /bɔrd/23/11; 52/2
boardwalk /bɔ́rdwɔk/35/9
body /bádi/8
boil /bɔil/66/22
bollard /bálərd/42/14
bolt /bolt/25/8; 28/4
bomb /bam/45/24
bomber /bámər/45/23
book /buk/18/14; 52/15
bookbag /búk-bæg/18/6
bookcase /búk-kes/21/24; 29/16
bookshelf /búk-šelf/50/25
boot /but/10/18; 13/3; 17/6
bottle /bátəl/32/33; 51/1; 67/5
bottle of wine /batəl-əv-wáin/51/25; 73/5
bottle opener /bátəl-opinər/30/23; 51/7
bottle top /bátəl-tap/51/2
bottom /bátəm/69/2
bough /bau/63/13
bow /báu/43/13; 49/6
bowl /bol/30/35; 73/14
bowl of soup /ból-əv-súp/73/14
box /baks/67/15; 73/10
boxer /báksər/46/11
box of cookies /báks-əv-kúkiz/73/2
box of matches /báks-əv-mǽčɪz/73/10
box of tissues /báks-əv-tíšuz/32/23
boxing /báksɪŋ/46
boxing glove /báksɪŋ-gləv/46/12
boy /bɔi/10
bra /bra/12/1
brace /bres/25/5
bracelet /bréslɪt/12/8
brain /bren/9/21
brake /brek/38/22; 40/14
brakeman /brekmən/41/10
branch /brænč/27/13; 63/13
bread /bred/20/19
breed box /bréd-baks/30/15
break /brek/64/2
breastbone /brést-bon/8/4
brick /brɪk/23/8
bricklayer /brík-leər/23/2
bridge /brɪj/14/12
bridle /brátdəl/46/5
briefcase /bríf-kes/11/28
broiler /brɔ́ilər/30/3
broom /brum/31/2
brother /bráðər/71/5
brother-in-law /bráðər-ɪn-lɔ/71/8
brush /brəš/12/20
bucket /bákət/31/19; 35/24
buckle /bákəl/10/17
bud /bəd/62/25
buffalo /báfəlo/56/8
building /bíldɪŋ/23
bulb /bálb/31/13
bull /bul/36/23
bullet /búlət/45/11
bulletin board /búlətɪn-bɔrd/21/10
bumper /bəmpər/38/6; 41/29
bunch /bənč/72/1
bunch of flowers /bánč-əv-fláuərz/72/1
bundle /bándəl/72/2
bundle of sticks /bándəl-av-stíks/72/2
Bunsen burner /bánsən-bárnər/19/12
buoy /búi/42/13
burner /bárnər/30/4
bus /bəs/15/24; 39/17
bush /buš/27/22
bus stop /bás-stap/15/25
butcher /búčər/54/2
butterfly /bátər-flai/59/25
buttocks /bátəks/8/19
button /bátən/11/26; 53/15
button hole /bátən-hol/53/16
by /bái/76/15

cab /kæb/40/22
cabbage /kǽbɪj/62/11
cabinet /kǽbɪnɪt/30/6
cable /kébəl/22/17; 37/4; 40/4; 42/15
cactus /kǽktəs/61/31
cake /kek/20/21
calculator /kǽlkyəletər/21/3
calendar /kǽləndər/18/20; 21/17; 70/11
calf /kæf/8/35; 36/22
calm /kam/75/4a
camel /kǽməl/56/6

camera /kǽmrə/**52**/25
camping /kǽmpɪŋ/**35**
campstove /kǽmp-stov/**35**/5
camping stove /kǽmpɪŋ-stov/**35**/5
can /kæn/**30**/22; **51**/4; **67**/7
canary /kənǽri/**60**/18
canned food /kǽnd-fúd/**20**/16
canoe /kənú/**43**/9
can-opener /kǽn-opənər/**30**/21
cap /kæp/**46**/9
capsule /kǽpsəl/**4**/19
captain /kǽptən/**44**/5
car /kar/**15**/30; **38**; **39**/16; **41**/4
car radio /kár-redio/**38**/25
carbon paper /kárbən-pepər/**21**/20
card /kard/**52**/10
card catalog /kárd-kætələg/**50**/23
card file /kárd-faɪl/**21**/26
cardigan /kárdɪgən/**10**/9
cargo /kárgo/**42**/6
Caribbean Sea /kærıbíən-si/**6**/18
carpenter /kárpɪntər/**54**/3
carpet /kárpɪt/**29**/3
carrot /kérət/**62**/5
carry /kéri/**64**/3
carry on case /kéri-an-kes/**67**/20
carton /kártən/**67**/1
cartridge /kártrɪj/**45**/11
cashier /kæšír/**20**/2
cash register /kǽš-rejɪstər/**20**/3
Caspian Sea /kǽspiən-sí/**6**/24
cast /kæst/**17**/27
castle /kǽsəl/**52**/4
cat /kæt/**56**/15
catch /kæč/**64**/4
catcher /kǽčər/**48**/5
catcher's mask /kǽčərz-mæsk/**48**/6
caterpillar /kǽtərpılər/**59**/27
cauliflower /káliflaʊər/**62**/10
cedar /sídər/**63**/23
ceiling /síliŋ/**29**/1
cell /sɛl/**16**/15
cello /čɛlo/**49**/8
cement /sɪmént/**23**/16
cement mixer /sɪmént-mɪksər/**23**/21
centigrade /séntıgred/**70**/12
centipede /séntıpid/**58**/22
center /séntər/**47**/15; **68**/20
center fielder /séntər fíldər/**48**/16
chain /čen/**40**/18; **47**/20
chair /čɛr/**29**/13; **30**/27
chalk /čɔk/**18**/4
chameleon /kəmíliən/**59**/3
changing table /čénjɪŋ-tebəl/**32**/32
check /čɛk/**51**/33
checkers /čɛkərz/**52**; **52**/9
checkout counter /čɛkaʊt-kaʊntər/**20**/4
cheek /čik/**9**/5
cheese /čiz/**20**/9
cherry /čéri/**61**/7
chess /čɛs/**52**
chess set /čɛs-sɛt/**52**/1
chest /čɛst/**8**/14
chest of drawers /čɛst-ə-drɔərz/**32**/16
chick /čık/**36**/35
chicken /číkın/**36**/33
children /čıldrın/**71**/2
chimney /čímni/**26**/2
chin /čın/**9**/6
chisel /čızəl/**24**/4
choke /čok/**38**/15
chop /čap/**66**/23
cigarette /sígərɛt/**51**/8
circle /sárkəl/**39**/4; **68**
circumference /sərkámfrəns/**68**/18
city /síti/**14–15**
clap /klæp/**66**/12
clarinet /klærınét/**49**/1
claw /klɔ/**58**/18
clean /klin/**74**/3a
clerk /klərk/**20**/8
cliff /klɪf/**35**/6
climb /klaɪm/**64**/5
clip /klɪp/**12**/23
clock-face /klák-fes/**70**/4
closed /klozd/**74**/4a
closet /klázət/**32**/14
cloth /klɔθ/**53**/13
clothes /kloz/**10–13**

clothesline /klóz-laın/**27**/28
clothespin /klóz-pın/**27**/30
cloud /klaʊd/**27**/2
clown /klaʊn/**54**/13
clutch /kləč/**38**/20
coach /koč/**41**/4
coastline /kóst-laın/**5**/11
coal /kol/**37**/3
coat /kot/**11**/14; **13**/11
coatrack /kót-ræk/**28**/9
cockpit /kákpıt/**45**/22
cockroach /kákroč/**59**/14
cocktail waitress /káktel-wetrıs/**51**/18
cocoa bean /kóko-bin/**63**/4
coconut /kókənət/**61**/9
cocoon /kəkún/**59**/28
coffee berry /kɔ́fi-beri/**63**/5
coffee pot /kɔ́fi-pat/**30**/20
coffee table /kɔ́fi-tebəl/**29**/23
coin /kɔ́ın/**20**/25
cold /kold/**74**/15b
cold water faucet /kold-wɔtər-fɔsıt/**33**/3
collar /kálər/**11**/2
collar bone /kálər-bon/**8**/2
comb /kom/**12**/19; **32**/22; **66**/12
combine (noun) /kámbaın/**36**/16
comet /kámət/**4**/1
common pin /kámən-pín/**53**/12
compact /kámpækt/**12**/12
compartment /kəmpártmınt/**41**/5
compass /kámpəs/**5**; **18**/11
conductor /kəndáktər/**41**/6; **49**/10
cone /kon/**63**/21; **68**/23
Congo /káŋgo/**7**/50
constellation /kánstəlésən/**4**/2
container /kənténər/**67**
continent /kántınənt/**6**
control panel /kəntról-pænəl/**45**/28
control tower /kəntról-taʊər/**44**/20
convertible /kənvártəbəl/**38**/38
cookie /kúki/**20**/20
cooling tower /kúlıŋ-taʊər/**37**/8
Coral Sea /kɔ́rəl-sí/**6**/29
cord /kɔrd/**28**/21; **31**/12
core /kɔr/**61**/4
cork /kɔrk/**51**/26
corkscrew /kɔ́rk-skru/**51**/11
corn /kɔrn/**63**/1
corner /kɔ́rnər/**69**/3
cottage /kátıj/**35**/8
cotton /kátən/**63**/6
couch /kaʊč/**29**/9
counter /káʊntər/**22**/3; **30**/8
country /kántri/**34**
court /kɔrt/**48**/23
court of law /kɔrt-əv-lɔ/**16**c
cousin /kázın/**71**/9
cover /kávər/**52**/16
cow /kaʊ/**36**/21
cowshed /káʊ-šed/**36**/3
crab /kræb/**58**/17
crackers /krǽkərz/**20**/26
crane /kren/**23**/1; **42**/4
crashhelmet /kræš-helmıt/**40**/27
crate /kret/**67**/17
crawl /krɔl/**64**/6
crescent moon /krésənt-mún/**4**/11
crest /krɛst/**60**/12
crib /krıb/**32**/26
cricket /kríkıt/**59**/11
crocodile /krákədaıl/**59**/1
crooked /krúkıd/**74**/5a
crossbar /krɔ́s-bar/**40**/15
crosswalk /krɔ́s-wɔk/**14**/2
crow /kro/**60**/33
crowd /kraʊd/**72**/3
crowd of people /kraʊd-əv-pipəl/**72**r
crutch /krəč/**17**/26
cry /kraı/**64**/7
crystal /krístəl/**19**/17
cube /kyub/**68**/24
cucumber /kyúkəmbər/**62**/8
cuff /kəf/**11**/3; **18**
cuff links /káf-lıŋks/**11**/25
cup /kəp/**30**/37; **73**/11
cup of coffee /kəp-əv-kɔfi/**73**/11
curb /kərb/**14**/8
curtain /kártən/**26**/14; **29**/7; **50**/6
curtain rod /kártən-rad/**33**/30

curve /kərv/**68**/3
cushion /kúšən/**29**/10
customer /kástəmər/**20**/5; **51**/23
customs /kástəmz/**44**/1
customs officer /kástəmz-ɔfısər/**44**/2
cut /kət/**64**/8
cylinder /sílındər/**68**/25
cylinder head /sílındər-hɛd/**38**/36
cymbal /símbəl/**49**/29

daffodil /dǽfədıl/**62**/17
daisy /dézi/**62**/18
dam /dæm/**37**/2
dance /dæns/**64**/9
Danube /dǽnyub/**7**/47
dark /dark/**75**/11b
dashboard /dáš-bɔrd/**38**/12
date /det/**61**/10; **70**
daughter /dɔ́tər/**71**/3
daughter-in-law /dɔ́tər-ın-lɔ/**71**/7
decimal point /désıməl-pɔ́ınt/**69**/21
deck /dɛk/**43**/19
deck chair /dɛ́k-čɛr/**35**/19
deck of cards /dɛ́k-əv-kárdz/**52**/10
deep /dip/**74**/6b
defense /dıféns/**45**
defendant /dıféndənt/**16**/20
defense attorney /dıféns-ətárni/**16**/21
degree /dıgrí/**70**/12
delta /délta/**5**/9
dental assistant /déntəl-əsıstənt/**17**/14
dentist /déntıst/**17**; **17**/16
dentist's chair /déntısts-čɛr/**17**/15
depth /dɛpθ/**69**/10
derrick /dérık/**37**/10
deserts /dézərts/**7**
desk /dɛsk/**18**/7; **21**/1; **32**/15; **50**/24
detection /dıtékšən/**16**
detergent /dətɔ́ryənt/**20**/28; **31**/18
diagonal /daıǽgənəl/**68**/15
dial /daıl/**19**/5; **28**/20
diameter /daıǽmətər/**68**/19
diaper /dáıpər/**32**/36
difficult /dífıkəlt/**74**/12b
dig /dıg/**64**/10
dirty /dárti/**74**/3b
dish towel /dıš-taʊəl/**30**/25
dish washer /díš-wɔšər/**30**/24
display window /dısplé-windo/**15**/21
distributor /dıstríbyutər/**38**/34
dive /daıv/**64**/11
diverter /dıvártər/**33**/7
divide by /dıváıd baı/**69**/18
dock /dak/**42**/12
doctor /dáktər/**17**/21; **55**/8
dog /dɔg/**56**/13
doll /dal/**32**/31
dolphin /dálfın/**57**/3
donkey /dɔ́ŋki/**56**/10
door /dɔr/**26**/7; **28**/1
doormat /dɔ́r-mæt/**26**/18; **28**/6
double bass /dábəl-bes/**49**/9
dove /dəv/**60**/24
down /daʊn/**76**/4
downstairs /dáʊnstérz/**28**/15
dragonfly /drǽgən-flaı/**59**/19
drain /dren/**14**/10; **33**/5
drainpipe /drén-paıp/**23**/9; **26**/17
drain plug /drén-pləg/**33**/6
draft beer /drǽft-bír/**51**/16
drape /drep/**29**/8
draw /drɔ/**64**/12
dream /drim/**64**/14
dress /drɛs/**13**/10
dressing table /drésıŋ-tebəl/**32**/10
dressing table skirt /drésıŋ-tebəl skərt/**32**/11
dressmaker /drés-mekər/**54**/10
drill /drıl/**17**/17
drink /drıŋk/**64**/13
drive /draıv/**64**/15
driver /dráıvər/**40**/25
drown /dráʊn/**64**/16
drum /drám/**49**/30
dry /draı/**74**/7b
duck /dək/**36**/32
duckling /dáklın/**36**/31
dump truck /dəmp-trək/**23**/22
dust brush /dást-brəš/**31**/6
dustcloth /dástklɔθ/**31**/7

dust pan /dʌ́st-pæn/31/8
eagle /ígəl/60/2
ear /ɪr/9/3
ear of corn /ír-əv-kórn/63/1
earring /ír-rɪŋ/12/9
Earth /árθ/4/7
east /ist/5/16
East China Sea /íst-čáɪnə-sí/7/32
easy /ízi/74/12a
eat /it/64/17
eclipse /iklíps/4/10
edge /ɛj/69/4
education /ɛjʊkéšən/18–19
eel /il/58/10
egg /ɛg/20/11
eggplant /ɛ́g-plænt/62/16
elastic /ɪlǽstɪk/53/7
elbow /ɛ́lbo/8/23
electric can opener /ɪléktrɪk-kǽn-opənər/30/19
electric drill /ɪléktrɪk-dríl/25/4
electric guitar /ɪléktrɪk-gɪtár/49/26
electrician /ɪlɛktríšən/55/2
elephant /ɛ́ləfənt/57/21
ellipse /ɪlíps/68
emergency brake /ɪmárjɪnsi-brek/38/19
empty /ɛ́mpti/74/8a
end table /ɛ́nd-tebəl/29/25
engine /ɛ́njɪn/38/31; 41/3
engineer /ɛnjɪnír/41/2
envelope /ɛ́nvəlop/21/11; 22/10, 15
equal /íkwəl/69/19
Equator /ɪkwétər/5/4
eraser /ɪrésər/18/3
estuary /ɛ́styʊɛri/5/10
Europe /yɔ́rəp/6/3
excavator /ɛ́kskəvetər/23/20
exhaust pipe /ɪgzɔ́st-paɪp/38/7; 40/35
expressway /ɪksprɛ́s-we/39/1
extension cord /ɪksténšən-kord/24/10
eye /áɪ/9/1
eyeball /áɪ-bɔl/9/15
eyebrow /áɪ-brau/9/16
eyelash /áɪ-læš/9/18
eyelid /áɪ-lɪd/9/17
eye shadow /áɪ-šædo/12/16

face /fes/9
face cream /fes-krim/12/17
Fahrenheit /fǽrɪnhaɪt/70/12
fall /fɔl/64/18
family /fǽmli/71
fare /fær/40/24
farm /farm/36
farmer /fármər/36/15
farm house /fárm-haus/36/7
fast /fæst/74/9a
fat /fæt/74/10a
father /fáðər/71/4
father-in-law /fáðər-ɪn-lɔ/71/6
feather /fɛ́ðər/60/5
feeler /fílər/59/16
fence /fɛns/36/10
fern /fərn/61/32
ferry /fɛ́ri/43/15
field /fild/34/13; 36/8; 47/6
field hockey /fíld-haki/46
fig /fɪg/61/29
fight /faɪt/64/19
fighter plane /fáɪtər-plen/45/21
figure /fígyər/68
file /faɪl/21/18; 24/2
file cabinet /fáɪl-kæbɪnɪt/21/19
filing cabinet /fáɪlɪŋ-kæbɪnɪt/21/19
film /film/52/24
fin /fɪn/57/4; 58/2
finger /fíŋgər/8/30
finger-nail /fíŋgər-nel/8/31
fingerprint /fíŋgər-prɪnt/16/11
fir /fər/63/20
fire /fáɪər/17; 17/12; 29/6
Fire Department /fáɪər-dɪpartmənt/17
fire engine /fáɪər-ɛnjɪn/17/7
fire escape /fáɪər-ɪskep/17/11
fire extinguisher /fáɪər-ɪkstɪngwɪšər/17/5
fire fighter /fáɪər-faɪtər/17/1
fire hose /fáɪər-hoz/17/3
fire hydrant /fáɪər-haɪdrənt/17/4
firefighter's boot /fáɪər-faɪtərz-bút/17/6

firefighter's hat /fáɪər-faɪtərz-hæt/17/2
fireplace /fáɪər-ples/29/4
fire truck /fáɪər-trək/17/7
first /fərst/75/10a
first base /fərst-bés/48/9
first baseman /fərst-bésmən/48/10
fish /fɪš/20/22; 58
fisherman /fíšərmən/48/18
fishing /fíšɪŋ/48
fishing rod /fíšɪŋ-rad/48/19
fist /fɪst/8/26
flag /flæg/41/11
flamingo /fləmíŋgo/60/8
flap /flæp/22/16
flashlight /flǽš-laɪt/16/9
flask /flæsk/19/16
fleet /flit/72/4
fleet of ships /flit-əv-šɪps/72/4
flight /flaɪt/72/5
flight attendant /fláɪt-əténdənt/44/7, 8
flight of stairs /fláɪt-əv-stǽrz/72/5
flipper /flɪpər/35/21; 57/10
flock /flak/72/6
flock of birds /flák-əv-bárdz/72/6
flock of sheep /flák-əv-šíp/72/6
floor /flɔr/28/7
florist /flɔ́rɪst/55/5
flower /fláuər/27/20; 62
flower bed /fláuər-bed/27/21
flower pot /fláuər-pat/27/24
fluke /fluk/57/2
fly /flaɪ/59/23; 64/20
foal /fol/56/2
folding rule /fóldɪŋ-rúl/24/12
foot /fʊt/8/37
football /fútbɔl/47; 47/1
footlights /fút-laɪts/50/13
footpath /fút-pæθ/34/17
footprint /fút-prɪnt/16/12
footrest /fút-rɛst/40/37
forearm /fɔ́r-arm/8/24
forehead /fɔ́r-hɛd/9/8
forest /fɔ́rɪst/34/9
fork /fɔrk/30/33
forklift /fɔ́rk-lɪft/42/17
foul line /fául-laɪn/48/14
foundations /faʊndéšənz/23/10
fox /faks/56/24
fraction /frǽkšən/69/22
freeway /frí-we/39/1
freezer /frízər/20/14
freight car /frét-kar/41/28
frog /frɔg/58/20
frond /frand/61/33
front /frənt/69/7
front door /frənt-dɔ́r/26/7
frown /fraun/66/14
fruit /fruit/20/17; 30/11; 61
fruit basket /frút-bæskɪt/30/10
fruit seller /frút-sɛlər/55/1
fruit tree /frút-tri/36/11
frying pan /fráɪŋ-pæn/30/14
full /fʊl/74/8b
full moon /fúl-mun/4/13
full back /fúl-bæk/47/10
furrow /fʌ́ro/36/20
fuselage /fyú:səlaž/44/10

galaxy /gǽləksi/4/3
gallery /gǽləri/50/9
game /gem/32/20
gang /gæŋ/72/7
gang of workmen /gǽŋ-əv-wárkmɪn/72/7
Ganges /gǽnjiz/7/52
gangway /gǽŋwe/42/10
garage /gəráž/26/6
garbage can /gárbɪj-kæn/30/9; 67/12
gardener /gárdnər/55/3
gas gauge /gǽs-gej/38/13
gas pump /gǽs-pəmp/39/8
gas station /gǽs-stešən/39/7
gas cap /gǽs-kæp/38/3
gate /get/27/16; 41/17
gateman /gét-mæn/41/16
gearshift /gír-šɪft/38/21; 40/38
gill /gɪl/58/5
giraffe /jərǽf/57/15
girl /gərl/12–13

give /gɪv/66/11
glass /glæs/30/36; 33/18; 51/27; 73/4
glasses /glǽsɪz/11/23
glider /gláɪdər/44/14
globe /glob/55
glove /gləv/11/20; 48/7
glue /glu/18/13
goalpost /gól-post/47/4,22
goat /got/36/24
Gobi /góbi/7/44
goggles /gágəlz/35/15; 40/28
good /gʊd/75/8a
goose /gus/60/25
gorilla /gərílə/57/14
gown /gáun/16/24
granddaughter /grǽn-dɔtər/71/12
grandson /grǽn-sən/71/12
grandstand /grǽnd-stænd/47/5
grape /grep/61/12
grapefruit /grép-frut/61/30
grass /græs/26/21
grasshopper /grǽshapər/59/12
grenade /grənéd/45/9
grill /grɪl/38/27
groundcloth /gráund-klɔθ/35/2
group /grup/72/11
group of tourists /grúp-əv-tərɪsts/72/11
guard /gard/16/13
guided missile /gáɪdɪd-mísəl/45/4
guitar /gɪtár/49/26
gulf /gəlf/6
Gulf of Alaska /gəlf-əv-əlǽskə/6/15
Gulf of Guinea /gəlf-əv-gíní/6/19
Gulf of Mexico /gəlf-əv-mɛ́ksɪko/6/17
gull /gəl/60/21
gun /gən/16/2; 45/6
gutter /gʌ́tər/14/9; 26/16

hacksaw /hǽk-sɔ/25/18
hair /hær/8/9
hairbrush /hær-brəš/32/21
hairdresser /hǽr-drɛsər/54/1
hair dryer /hǽr-draɪər/31/14
half /hæf/69/2
half moon /hǽf-mún/4/12
hall /hɔl/28
hammer /hǽmər/25/14
hamper /hǽmpər/33/28
hand /hænd/8/27
hand brake /hǽnd-brek/38/19
handcuffs /hǽn-kəfs/16/8
hand drill /hǽn-drɪl/25/3
hand grenade /hǽn-grənéd/45/9
handkerchief /hǽŋkərčif/13/9
handle /hǽndəl/25/16
handlebars /hǽndəl-barz/40/6
hangar /hǽŋər/44/21
happy /hǽpi/74/11a
hard /hard/74/13b
hard liquor /hárd-líkər/51/17
hat /hæt/11/13
hatchet /hǽčɪt/25/7
hawk /hɔk/60/6
hay /he/36/2
hayloft /hé-lɔft/36/1
head /hɛd/8/10; 25/15
headboard /hɛ́d-bord/32/2
headlight /hɛ́d-laɪt/38/29; 40/5
heart /hart/9/23
heavy /hɛ́vi/75/12b
hedge /hɛj/27/17; 34/14
hedgehog /hɛj-hɔg/56/26
heel /hil/9/38; 11/11
height /haɪt/69/9
helicopter /hɛ́lɪkaptər/44/15
helmet /hɛlmɪt/47/2
hem /hɛm/53/4
hen /hɛn/36/33
herd /hərd/72/10
herd of cattle /hərd-əv-kætəl/72/10
hero /híron/60/15
herring /hɛ́rɪŋ/58/6
hibiscus /haɪbískəs/62/24
high /haɪ/74/14a
highway /haíwe/39/11
hill /hɪl/34/10
Himalayas /hɪməléəz/7/40
hinge /hɪnj/28/5
hip /hɪp/8/18

hip-bone /híp-bon/**8**/7
hippopotamus /hɪpəpátəməs/**57**/20
hit /hɪt/**66**/5
hobby /hábi/**52**
hod /had/**23**/18
hold /hold/**42**/8; **66**/20
hole puncher /hól-pənčər/**21**/6
hollow /hálo/**75**/14b
homeplate /hom-plét/**48**/4
hood /hud/**38**/26
hoof /huf/**36**/27
hook /huk/**28**/10; **48**/21
hook and eye /húk-ən-aí/**53**/23
horizon /həráɪzən/**42**/1
horn /hɔrn/**49**/14; **56**/9; **57**/26
horse /hɔrs/**36**/25; **46**/2; **56**/1
horse-racing /hɔ́rs-resɪŋ/**46**
hose /hoz/**17**/3
hospital bed /háspɪtəl-bed/**17**/19
hospital ward /háspɪtəl-wɔrd/**17**
hot /hat/**74**/15a
hot dog /hát-dɔg/**20**/12
hotel /hotél/**35**/7
hot water faucet /hát-wɔ́tər-fɔsɪt/**33**/2
hour hand /áuər-hænd/**70**/2
house /háus/**26**
household /háus-hold/**31**
hubcap /háb-kæp/**38**/30
Hudson Bay /hádsən-bé/**6**/16
hug /həg/**66**/6
human /hyúmən/**8**
hummingbird /hə́mɪŋ-bərd/**60**/27
hump /həmp/**56**/7
husband /házbənd/**71**/1
hydrant /háɪdrənt/**17**/4
hypoteneuse /haɪpátənus/**68**/12

icecream /áɪs-krím/**35**/17
ice skater /áɪs-sketər/**47**/30
ice skates /áɪs-skets/**47**/31
icicle /áɪsɪkəl/**27**/8
ignition /ɪgníšən/**38**/14
illustration /ɪləstréšən/**52**/20
in /ɪn/**76**/10
in box /ín-baks/**21**/12
Indian /índiən/**6**/13
Indus /índəs/**7**/51
in front of /ɪn-fránt-əv/**76**/7
insect /ínsekt/**59**
inside /ɪnsáɪd/**76**/10
inside lane /ínsaɪd-lén/**39**/6
insides /ɪnsáɪdz/**9**
instep /ínstep/**9**/39
intersection /íntərsekšən/**14**/15
intestines /ɪntéstɪnz/**9**/27
into /ɪn-tu/**76**/9
iris /áɪrɪs/**9**/20
iron /áɪərn/**31**/11; **66**/18
ironing board /áɪərnɪŋ-bɔrd/**31**/3
irrigation canal /ɪrɪgéšən-kənæl/**36**/17
island /áɪlənd/**5**/12

jack of clubs /jæk-əv-kləbz/**52**/11
jacket /jǽkɪt/**10**/7, 19; **11**/27;
    13/7; 29/22; **52**/17
jail /jel/**16**
jar /jar/**67**/6
jaw /jɔ/**9**/9
jeans /jinz/**10**/14; 13/14
jeep /jip/**45**/5
jellyfish /jéli-fɪš/**58**/11
jet engine /jét-énjɪn/**44**/12
jewelry box /juəlri-baks/**32**/24
jigger /jígər/**51**/34
jockey /jáki/**46**/1
jodhpurs /jádpərz/**46**/8
judge /jəj/**16**/22
judo /júdo/**46**
judo suit /júdo sut/**46**/23
jump /jəmp/**64**/21
jury /jɔ́ri/**16**/17

Kalahari /kaləhári/**7**/42
kangaroo /kæŋgərú/**57**/6
keel /kil/**43**/5
kettle /kétəl/**30**/17
key /ki/**49**/16
kick /kɪk/**64**/22

kidney /kídni/**9**/26
king /kɪŋ/**52**/8
kingfisher /kíŋfɪšər/**60**/30
king of hearts /kíŋ-əv-hárts/**52**/13
kiss /kɪs/**66**/7
kitchen /kíčɪn/**30**
kite /káɪt/**35**/30
kitten /kítən/**56**/16
knee /ni/**8**/34
kneecap /ní-kæp/**8**/8
kneesock /ní-sak/**13**/12
kneel /nil/**64**/23
knife /náɪf/**30**/15
knight /náɪt/**52**/5
knitting /nítɪŋ/**53**/21
knitting needle /nítɪŋ-nidəl/**53**/18

lab /læb/**19**
label /lébəl/**22**/21
laboratory /lǽbrətori/**19**
lace /les/**53**/9
ladder /lǽdər/**17**/8; **23**/5
lake /lek/**5**/13; **34**/5
lamb /læm/**36**/30
lamp /læmp/**17**/18; **29**/26
lamp shade /lǽmp-šed/**29**/27
lapel /ləpél/**11**/15
large /larj/**74**/1a
last /læst/**75**/10b
laugh /læf/**64**/24
launch pad /lɔ́nč-pæd/**4**/17
launching pad /lɔ́nčɪŋ-pæd/**4**/17
laundry /lɔ́ndri/**27**/29
law /lɔ/**16**
lawn /lɔn/**27**/19
lawyer /lɔ́ɪyər/**16**/21/ **16**/23
leaf /lif/**63**/15
leap /lip/**64**/21
leaves /livz/**27**/15
left end /left-énd/**47**/18
left fielder /léft-fildər/**48**/15
left guard /left-gárd/**47**/16
left halfback /left-hǽlf-bæk/**47**/11
left lane /læft-lén/**39**/5
left tackle /læft-tǽkəl/**47**/17
leg /lɛg/**8**/32
leisure /léžər/**50**
lemon /lémən/**61**/14
length /lɛŋkθ/**69**/11
lens /lɛnz/**19**/10; **52**/26
leopard /lépərd/**57**/18
lettuce /létəs/**62**/12
level /lévəl/**23**/9
librarian /laɪbrǽriən/**50**/22
library /láɪbrǽri/**50**
license plate /láɪsəns-plet/**38**/28
lichee /líči/**61**/26
lick /lɪk/**64**/25
lie /láɪ/**65**/3
light /láɪt/**17**/18; **28**/16; **47**/7; **75**/11a, 12a
light aircraft /láɪt-ǽrkræft/**44**/17
light-bulb /láɪt-bəlb/**31**/13
lighter /láɪtər/**51**/14
lightning /láɪtnɪŋ/**27**/1
light-switch /láɪt-swɪč/**28**/17
line /láɪn/**48**/20; **68**;
line of latitude /láɪn-əv-lætɪtud/**5**/15
line of longitude /láɪn-əv-lɔnjɪtud/**5**/14
linesman /láɪnzmən/**47**/21
line-up /láɪn-əp/**47**
lion /láɪən/**57**/16
lip /lɪp/**9**/13
lipstick /lípstɪk/**12**/18
listen /lísən/**65**/1
little /lítəl/**74**/16
liver /lívər/**9**/25
living-room /lívɪŋ-rum/**29**
lizard /lízərd/**59**/9
llama /láмə/**56**/5
loaf /lof/**73**/6
loafer /lófər/**10**/10 /
loaf of bread /lof-əv-bréd/**73**/6
lobster /lábstər/**58**/12
lock /lak/**28**/3
locust /lókəst/**59**/10
log /lɔg/**63**/18
long /lɔŋ/**74**/16a
longshoreman /lɔ́ŋ-šórmən/**54**/6
loose /lus/**75**/16a

loose-leaf notebook /lús-lif-not-buk/**18**/18
loose-leaf paper /lús-lif-pépər/**18**/17
loud /láud/**75**/13a
loudspeaker /láud-spikər/**49**/28
low/lo/**74**/14b
luggage /lə́gɪj/**44**/4
luggage rack /lǽgɪj-ræk/**41**/9
lump /ləmp/**73**/7
lump of sugar /ləmp-əv-šúgər/**73**/7
lung /ləŋ/**9**/24

machine gun /məšín-gən/**45**/15
magazine /mǽgəzin/**29**/15
magazine rack /mǽgəzin-ræk/**29**/14
magnet /mǽgnət/**19**/19
magnifying-glass /mǽgnɪfaɪɪŋ-glæs/**16**/10
mailbag /mél-bæg/**22**/6
mailbox /mél-baks/**14**/1; **22**/4
mail carrier /mél-kæriər/ **22**/5
mail slot /mél-slat/**28**/2
mallet /mǽlət/**25**/1
mane /men/**36**; **57**/17
mango /mǽngo/**61**/15
mantel /mǽntəl/**29**/5
mantis /mǽntɪs/**59**/15
map /mæp/**5**; **18**/19
mascara /mæskǽrə/**12**/13
mask /mæsk/**35**/15
mast /mæst/**43**/3
mat /mæt/**28**/6
match /mæč/**51**/6
match book /mǽč-baks/**51**/5
material /mətíriəl/**53**/13
mattress /mǽtrɪs/**32**/8
meadow /médo/**34**/11
measurement /méžərmənt/**69**
meat /mit/**20**/13
mechanic /məkǽnɪk/**54**/5
medical /médɪkəl/**17**
medicine chest /médɪsɪn-čest/**33**/11
Mediterranean Sea /meditərénɪən-sí/**6**/22
Mekong /mékɔŋ/**7**/53
men /mɛn/**10**
menu /ményu/**51**/24
messy /mési/**75**/7b
meter /mítər/**19**/4; **40**/23
microphone /maɪkrəfon/**49**/25
microscope /maɪkrəskop/**19**/9
milk /mɪlk/**20**/10
miner /máɪnər/**54**/7
minus /máɪnəs/**69**/17
minute hand /mínɪt-hænd/**70**/1
mirror /mírər/**32**/13; **40**/3
Mississippi /mɪsɪsípi/**7**/45
mitt /mɪt/**48**/7
money order /máni-ɔrdər/**22**/18
monkey /máŋki/**57**/12
monkey wrench /máŋki-renč/**24**/9
Moon /mun/**4**/6
mop /map/**31**/5
mortar /mórtər/**19**/21
mosquito /məskíto/**59**/20
moth /mɔθ/**59**/26
mother /máðər/**71**/4
mother-in-law /máðər-ɪn-lɔ/**71**/6
motorboat /mótər-bot/**35**/34; **43**/11
motorcycle /mótər-saɪkəl/**14**/16; **39**/20
mountain /máuntən/**34**/2
mountain peak /máuntən pik/**34**/3
mountain range /mauntən-renj/**7**
mouse /máus/**56**/18
mouth /máuθ/**9**/4
mouthpiece /máuθ-pis/**49**/23
movie theater /múvi-θitər/**50**/17
movies /múviz/**50**
mudguard /mə́d-gard/**40**/10
mug /məg/**51**/3
multiply by /mə́ltɪplaɪ baɪ/**69**/16
muscle /mə́səl/**9**/31
mushroom /mə́šrum/**62**/14
music /myúzɪk/**49**; **49**/12
musician /myuzíšən/**49**/3
mustache /məstǽš/**9**/10

nail /nel/**8**/31; **25**/11
nail-file /nél-faɪl/**12**/11
nail-brush /nél-braš/**33**/20
nail polish /nél-palɪš/**12**/14
napkin /nǽpkɪn/**30**/28; **51**/32

napkin holder /nǽpkɪn-holdər/30/29
narrow /nǽro/75/1a
national defense /nǽšənəl-dífɛns/45
navigator /nǽvɪgetər/45/26
Navy /névi/45
near /nɪr/76/15
neat /nit/75/7a
neck /nɛk/8/11
necklace /nɛkləs/12/10
needle /nídəl/5/16; 53/6; 63/22
negative /négətɪv/52/23
nephew /néfyu/71/11
nest /nɛst/60/29
net /nɛt/46/20; 48/24
new /nu/75/3a
new moon /nú-mún/4/11
newspaper /núz-pepər/29/12
next to /nékst-tu/76/14
niece /nis/71/11
Niger /náɪjər/7/49
nightgown /náɪt-gaun/12/5
night table /náɪt-tebəl/32/9
nightstick /náɪt-stɪk/16/7
Nile /naɪl/7/48
nipple /nípəl/32/34
north /nɔrθ/5/16
North America /nɔrθ-əmérɪkə/6/1
North Atlantic /nɔrθ-ətlǽntɪk/6/11
northeast /nɔrθ-íst/5/16
North Pacific /nɔrθ-pəsífɪk/6/9
North Pole /nɔrθ-pól/5/1
North Sea /nɔrθ-sí/6/20
northwest /nɔrθ-wést/5/16
nose /noz/9/2
nosecone /nóz-kon/4/15
notebook /nót-buk/18/18
noun /náun/72; 73
nozzle /názəl/17/9
nurse /nərs/17/25; 55/10
nut /nət/25/13
nutmeat /nát-mit/61/28

oar /ɔr/43/7
oarlock /ɔ́r-lak/43/8
oak tree /ók-tri/63/10
objects /ábjɛkts/31
oblong /áblɔŋ/68
obtuse angle /əbtús-ǽŋgəl/68/10
occupation /akyupéšən/54–55
ocean /óšən/6
ocean liner /óšən-laɪnər/43/20
o'clock /əklák/70/5
octopus /áktəpəs/58/23
off /ɔf/77/6
office /ɔ́fɪs/21
office building /ɔ́fɪs-bɪldɪŋ/15/19
oil-rig /ɔ́ɪl-rɪg/37/11
oil truck /ɔ́ɪl-trək/39/19
old /old/75/2b, 3b
old moon /óld-mún/4/14
olive /álɪv/63/3
on /an/76/12, 13
onion /ányən/62/13
onto /an-tu/76/13
open /ópən/65/2; 74/4b
operator /ápəretər/21/16
optician /aptíšən/55/14
orange /ɔ́rənj/61/16
orbit /ɔ́rbɪt/4/9
orchard /ɔ́rčərd/36/12
orchestra /ɔ́rkəstrə/49; 50/11
orchestra pit /ɔ́rkəstrəpɪt/50/12
orchid /ɔ́rkɪd/62/21
ostrich /ástrič/60/1
out of /áut-əv/76/11
outboard motor /áutbɔrd-mótər/43/12
outlet /áut-lɛt/31/16
outside /áutsáɪd/76/1
outside-lane /áutsaɪd-lén/39/5
outside wall /áutsaɪd-wɔ́l/26/3
oval /óvəl/68
oven /ávən/30/2
overcoat /óvər-kot/11/14
overpass /óvər-pæs/39/2
owl /ául/60/7
oyster /ɔ́ɪstər/58/16

pacifier /pǽsɪfaɪər/32/28
pack /pǽk/73/10

pack of cigarettes /pǽk-əv-sɪgərɛts/73/10
package /pǽkɪj/22/19
paddle /pǽdəl/43/10
page /pej/52/19
pail /pel/31/19; 35/24
paint /pent/65/4
paintbrush /pént-brəš/24/14
paint can /pént-kæn/24/17
paint pan /pént-pæn/24/16
paint roller /pént-rolər/24/15
pajamas /pəjáməz/10/2
palm /pam/8/28; 63/19
pan /pæn/19/2; 24/16; 30/13
panties /pǽntiz/12/3
pants /pǽnts/11/17
pantsuit /pǽnt-sut/13/2
pantyhose /pǽnti-hoz/12/4
papaya /pəpáɪə/61/25
paper bag /pepər-bǽg/67/2
paper clip /pépər-klɪp/21/9
paper cup /pepər-káp/67/8
parachute /pǽrəšut/45/25
parallel lines /pǽrəlɛl-láɪnz/68/5
park /park/14/11
parking lot /párkɪŋ-lat/15/29
parking meter /párkɪŋ-mitər/15/23
parrakeet /pǽrəkit/60/26
parrot /pǽrət/60/20
pass /pǽs/66/13
passenger /pǽsɪnjər/40/26; 41/19; 44/6
passport /pǽs-pɔrt/44/3
path /pæθ/27/18; 34/17
patient /péšənt/17/20
patio /pǽtio/26/5
pattern /pǽtərn/53/20
paw /pɔ/56/17
pawn /pɔn/52/3
pea /pi/62/3
peach /pič/61/19
peacock /pí-kak/60/11
peak /pik/34/3
peanut /pí-nət/61/11
pear /per/61/22
pebble /pɛbəl/35/28
pedal /pédəl/40/17, 49/17
peel /pil/61/6, 18
pelvis /pélvɪs/8/7
pen /pɛn/18/9; 36/5
pencil /pénsəl/18/8
pencil holder /pénsəl-holdər/21/27
penguin /péngwɪn/60/13
pepper mill /pépər-mɪl/51/29
pepper shaker /pépər-šekər/30/40; 51/30
per cent /pər-sént/69/20
perfume /pɔ́rfyum/12/15
periscope /pérɪskop/45/20
perpendicular line /pərpɪndíkyulər laɪn/68/4
Persian Gulf /pɔ́ržən-gəlf/6/26
pestle /péstəl/19/20
petal /pétəl/62/20
phase /féz/4
pheasant /fézənt/60/14
photo /fóto/52/22
photocopier /fóto-kapiər/21/14
photograph /fótəgræf/52/22
photographer /fətágrəfər/55/4
photography /fətágrəfi/52
piano /piǽno/49/15
pick /pɪk/66/8
pick(ax) /pík-æks/23/12
piece /pis/73/8
piece of cake /pis-əv-kek/73/8
pier /pɪr/42/2
pig /pɪg/56/3
pigeon /píjən/60/31
pile /páɪl/72/9, 12
pile of blankets /páɪl-əv-blǽŋkits/72/12
pile of stones /páɪl-əv-stónz/72/9
pillow /pílo/32/3
pillowcase /pílo-kes/32/4
pilot /páɪlət/44/5; 45/27
pin /pɪn/53/12
pincer /pínsarz/58/18
pineapple /páɪnæpəl/61/24
pinecone /páɪn-kon/63/21
pine needles /páɪn-nidəlz/63/22
ping-pong /píŋ-pɔŋ/46
pip /pɪp/61/20
pipeline /páɪp-laɪn/37/12

pipette /paɪpét/19/18
pistol /pístəl/45/10
pit /pɪt/50/12; 61/8; 20
pitcher /pičər/48/8
pitchfork /pič-fɔrk/27/25
placemat /plés-mæt/30/30
plane /plen/25/2; 44/9
planet /plǽnɪt/4/4
plant /plǽnt/61–63
plastic wrap /plǽstɪk-ræp/67/10
plate /plet/30/34; 72/13
plate of sandwiches /plet-əv-sǽndwɪčɪz/72/13
plateau /plǽto/34/1
platform /plǽtfɔrm/41/20
platform number /plǽfɔrm-nəmbər/41/21
player /pléər/49/3
pleat /plit/53/11
pliers /pláɪərz/25/19
plow /pláu/36/19
plug /pləg/31/15
plum /pləm/61/23
plus /pləs/69/15
pneumatic drill /numǽtɪk-dríl/23/23
pocket /pákət/11/16
pocketknife /pákət-naif/24/5
pod /pad/62/4
pointer /pɔ́ɪntər/19/6
pole /pol/47/27
Pole /pol/5/A.1.7
police car /pəlís-kar/16/5
police dog /pəlís-dɔg/16/11
police officer /pəlis-ɔfgsər/16/1; 55/13
police station /pəlís-stešən/16/4
pond /pand/34/19; 36/9
pop group /páp-grup/49
porter /pɔ́rtər/54/14
postcard /póst-kard/22/19
postmark /póst-mark/22/8
post office /póst-ɔfis/22
postal clerk /póstəl-klərk/22/1
pot /pat/30/12
potato /pətéto/20/27; 62/6
pouch /páuč/57/7
power /páuər/37
powerhouse /páuər-haus/37/3
power saw /páuər-sɔ/24/11
power station /páuər-stešən/37/6
preposition /prepəzíšən/76–77
pretty /príti/75/9a
prisoner /prízənər/16/14
profession /prəféšən/54; 55
projectionist /prəjékšənɪst/50/16
projection room /prəjékšən-rum/50/14
projector /prəjéktər/50/15; 52/29
propeller /prəpélər/44/18
prosecuting attorney /prásɪkyutɪŋ-ətɔ́rtni/16/23
protractor /prótræktər/18/12
pull /pul/65/5
pump /pəmp/40/16
pupil /pyúpəl/9/19
puppy /pápi/56/14
purse /pərs/13/4
push /puš/65/6
put /put/66/15
pylon /páɪlan/37/5
pyramid /pírəmɪd/68/22

quantity /kwántɪti/72
quarter /kwɔ́rtər/69/14
quarterback /kwɔ́rtə-bæk/47/8
queen /kwin/52/7
queen of diamonds /kwín-əv-dáɪəməndz/52/12

rabbit /rǽbɪt/56/20
racehorse /rés-hɔrs/46/2
racing /résɪŋ/46
rack /ræk/28/9
racket /rǽkɪt/46/19; 48/27
radiator /rédietər/38/33
radio /redio/29/24
radius /rédɪəs/68/17
rafter /rǽftər/23/3
railroad switch /rélrod-swič/41/26
railroad ties /rélrod-taɪz/41/25
railroad track /rélrod-træk/41/24
rain /ren/27/3
raincoat /rén-kot/11/12

raindrop /rén-drap 27/4
rainhat /rén-hæt 11/30
rat /ræt/56/22
rattle /rǽtəl/32/30
razor /rézər/33/13
razor-blade /rézər-bled/33/14
read /rid/65/7
reading /rídiŋ/52
rear light /rír-láit/40/30
rearview mirror /rır-vyu-mírər/38/1
receipt /rısít/20/23
receiver /rısívər/28/19
receptionist /rısépšənıst/21/25
record /rékərd/29/21
record jacket /rékərd-jækət/29/22
recreation /rekriešən/46–52
rectangle /réktæŋəl/68
Red Sea /réd-sí/6/25
referee /referí/46/10; 47/3
refinery /rıfáınəri/37/13
reflector /rıfléktər/40/20
refrigerator /rıfríjəretər/30/5
reindeer /réndır/56/11
reins /renz/46/4
relationship /rıléšənšıp/71
reptile /réptaıl/59
reservoir /rézəvwar/37/1
restaurant /réstərant/51
return address /rıtórn-ædrɛs/22/12
revolver /rıválvər/45/12
rhinoceros /raınásərəs/57/25
rib /rıb/8/5
ribbon /ríbən/53/24
rice /ráıs/63/7
ride /ráıd/65/8
rifle /ráıfəl/45/2
right angle /ráıt-æŋgəl/68/14
right end /raıt-énd/47/12
right fielder /ráıt-fíldər/48/17
right guard /raıt-gárd/47/14
right halfback /raıt-hǽf-bæk/47/9
right lane /raıt-lén/39/6
right tackle /raıt-tǽkəl/47/13
rind /raınd/61/18
ring /rıŋ/12/7; 46/13
river /rívər/7; 34/12
road /rod/15/31; 34/18; 38–40
robe /rob/16/24
rock /rak/35/29
rocket /rákət/4/16
Rockies /rákiz/7/36
rod /rad/48/19
roll /rol/73/12
roller /rólər/12/22; 24/15
roll of film /ról-əv-fílm/52/24
roll of paper /ról-əv-pépər/73/12
roof /ruf/26/1
rook /ruk/52/4
rooster /rústər/36/34
root /rut/63/11
rope /rop/46/14
rose /roz/62/19
rostrum /rástrəm/49/13
rotor /rótər/44/16
rough /rəf/75/4b, 5a
row /rol/72/14
row of houses /ró-əv-hóuzız/72/14
rowboat /ró-bot/43/6
rubber boot /rábər-bút/10/12
rubber tubing /rábər-túbıŋ/19/14
rudder /rádər/43/4
ruffle /rəfəl/53/14
rug /rəg/28/8; 32/17
ruler /rúlər/18/10
run /rən/65/9
rung /rəŋ/23/6
runway /rónwe/44/19

sad /sæd/72/11b
saddle /sǽdəl/36/28; 46/3
saddlebag /sǽdəl-bæg/40/8, 34
safety belt /séfti-belt/38/24
safety pin /séfti-pın/53/10
Sahara /səhæ̀rə/7/41
sail /sel/43/2; 65/10
sailboat /sél-bot/43/1
sailor /sélər 55/15
salesman /sélzmən/55/9

salesperson/ sélzpərsən/55/19
salmon /sǽmən/58/4
saltshaker /sólt-šekər/30/39; 51/28
sand /sænd/23/15; 35/22
sandal /sǽndəl/13/17
sandcastle /sǽnd-kæsəl/35/23
sandpaper /sǽnd-pepər/24/3
sandwich bag /sǽnwıč-bæg/67/4
satellite /sǽtəlaıt/4/18
saw /sɔ/25/17
saxophone /sǽksıfon/49/22
scaffolding /skǽfaldıŋ/23/7
scale /skel/22/2; 33/24; 59/7
scales /skelz/19/1; 58/9
scarecrow /skǽr-kro/36/13
scarf /skarf/11/19
schedule /skéjəl/41/15
school /skul/18
science /sáıəns/19
scissors /sízərz/53/26
scooter /skútər/40/29
scoreboard /skɔr-bórd/47/23
scorpion /skórpıən/58/27
scouring powder /skáurıŋ-paudər/31/9
screen /skrin/50/18; 52/27
screw /skru/25/9
screwdriver /skrú-draıvər/24/7
scrub brush /skráb-brəš/31/10
sea /si/6–7; 35
seagull /sí-gəl/60/21
Sea of Japan /sí-əv-jəpǽn/7/33
Sea of Okhotsk /sí-əv-okátsk/7/34
seal /sil/57/9
seam /sim/53/3
seam binding /sim-baındıŋ/ 532
seamstress /simstrəs/54/10
seashell /sí-šel/35/27
seaside /sí-saıd/35
seat /sit/38/23; 40/7, 30; 41/8; 50/20
seat-belt /sít-belt/38/24
seawall /sí-wɔl/35/10
seaweed /sí-wid/35/37
second hand /sékənd-hænd/70/3
second baseman /sekənd-bésmən/48/11
secretary /sékrətæri/21/22
section /sékšən/61/17; 68/21
sedan /sıdǽn/38/37
seed /sid/62/28
server /sávər/48/25
service /sárvıs/17
service line /sárvıs-laın/48/26
set /sɛt/50/4
sew /so/65/11
sewer /súər/14/10
sewing /sóıŋ/53
sewing machine /sóıŋ-məšin/53/1
shallow /šǽlo/74/6a
shape /šep/68
shark /šark/58/1
sharp /šarp/74/2b
shaving brush /šévıŋ-brəš/33/16
shaving mug /šévıŋ-məg/33/15
shed /šed/26/20; 27/26
sheep /šip/36/29
sheet /šit/32/5
sheet music /šít-myuzık/49/12
shelf /šelf/20/15; 24/18; 29/17; 30/16
shell /šel/45/7; 58/14; 59/5
shingle /šıŋgəl/23/4
ship /šıp/42/7
shirt /šərt/11/1; 13/15
shoe /šu/10/11; 11/8
shoelace /šú-les/11/9
shoot /šut/65/12
shopping bag /šápıŋ-bæg/67/18
shopping basket /šápıŋ-bæskıt/20/7
shopping cart /šápıŋ-kart/20/1
short /šɔrt/74/16b
shorts /šɔrts/10/5
shortstop /šórt-stap/48/12
shoulder /šóldər/8/13
shoulder bag /šóldər-bæg/13/4
shoulder-blade /šóldər-bled/8/3
shovel /šávəl/23/13; 35/25
shower curtain /šáuər-kərtən/33/31
shower head /šáuər-hed/33/4
shut /šət/65/13; 74/4a
shutter /šátər/26/12
side /saıd/68/13; 69/5

sidewalk /sáıd-wɔk/15/26
siding /sáıdıŋ 41/30
signal /sígnəl/41/27
signal box /sígnəl-baks/41/23
signalman /sígnəlmən/41/22
sill /sıl/26/11
sing /sıŋ/65/14
singer /síŋər/49/24
sink /sıŋk/30/7; 33/12
sister /sístər/71/5
sister-in-law /sístər-in-lɔ/71/8
sit /sıt/65/15
site /sáıt/23
sixteenth /sıkstínθ/70/11
skate /sket/47/31
skater /sketər/47/30
skeleton /skélətən/8
ski /ski/47/26
skier /skíər/47/25
skillet /skílıt/30/14
skin /skın/61/3
ski-pole /skí-pol/47/27
skirt /skərt/13/8
skull /skəl/8/1
sky /skáı/27/10
slacks /slæks/10/8; 11/17; 11/29
sleep /slip/66/19
sleeper /slípər/32/27
sleeping bag /slípıŋ-bæg/35/3
sleeve /sliv/11/7
slide /sláıd/19/11; 49/21; 52/30
slide projector /sláıd-prəjektər/52/29
slide rule /sláıd-rul/18/16
sling /slıŋ/17/23
slip /slıp/12/2
slipper /slípər/10/3; 12/6
sloppy /slápi/75/7b
slow /slo/74/9b
slug /sləg/58/19
small /smɔl/74/1b
smile /smaıl/65/16
smoke /smok/17/13
smokestack /smók-stæk/37/7; 42/9; 43/21
smooth /smuð/75/5b
snail /snel/58/13
snake /snek/59/6
snap /snæp/53/27
sneaker /sníkər/10/13
snorkel /snórkəl/35/16
snout /snáut/56/4; 58/8
snow /sno/27/5
snowball /snó-bɔl/27/6
snowman /snó-mæn/27/7
soap /sop/33/27
soap powder /sóp-paudər/20/28; 31/18
sock /sak/10/6; 13/12
socket /sákıt/31/16
sofa /sófə/29/9
soft /sɔft/74/13a; 75/13b
softdrink /sɔ́ft-drínk/51/13
soldier /sóljər/45/1; 55/12
sole /sol/9/40; 11/10
solid /sálıd/75/14a
solid figures /sálıd-fígyərz/68
son /sən/71/3
son-in-law /sán-ın-lɔ/71/7
south /sauθ/5/16
South America /sauθ-əmérıkə/6/2
South Atlantic /sauθ-ətlǽntık/6/12
South China Sea /sáuθ-čáınə-sí/7/31
southeast /sáuθ-íst/5/16
Southern /sáðərn/6/14
South Pacific /sauθ-pəsífık/6/10
South Pole /sáuθ-pól/5/7
southwest /sáuθ-wést/5/16
space /spes/4
space-capsule /spés-kæpsəl/4/19
spacesuit /spés-sut/4/21
space-travel /spés-trævəl 4
spark plug /spárk-pləg 38/35
sparrow /spǽro 60/28
speaker /spíkər 29/20; 49/28
speedometer /spidámətər 38/16
spider /spáıdər 58/25
spider web /spáıdər-web 58/26
spin /spın/66/16
spine /spáın 8/6; 52/18
spiral /spáırəl 68/1

spoke /spok/ **40**/12
sponge /spənj/ **33**/26
spool of thread /spul/((əv θréd/) **53**/8; **73**/9
spoon /spun/ **30**/32
sport /sport/ **46–48**
sportcoat /spórt-kot/ **10**/7; **11**/27
sports car /spórts-kar/ **39**/18
sports coupe /spórts-kup/ **38**/39
spotlight /spát-laɪt/ **50**/7
sprocket /sprákɪt/ **40**/19
square /skwær/ **68**
squash /skwaš/ **62**/7
squirrel /skwórəl/ **56**/19
stadium /stédiəm/ **47**
stage /stej/ **50**/1
stair /stɛr/ **28**/11
staircase /stérkes/ **28**/12
stalk /stɔk/ **61**/2; **62**/2
stamp /stæmp/ **22**/9
stand /stænd/ **47**/5; **52**/28; **65**/17
stapler /stéplər/ **21**/7
star /star/ **4**/5
starter /stártər/ **40**/36
station /stéšən/ **41**/13
station wagon /stešən-wægən/ **38**/40
stein /staɪn/ **51**/3
steering wheel /stíriŋ-hwil/ **38**/17
stem /stɛm/ **62**/23
stenographer /stənɔ́grəfər/ **16**/25
steno pad /sténo-pæ/ **21**/23
stern /stərn/ **43**/14
stethoscope /stéθəskop/ **17**/22
stick /stɪk/ **46**/18
stir /stər/ **65**/18
stirrup /stárəp/ **46**/7
stitch /stɪč/ **53**/17
stomach /stáмək/ **8**/17
stool /stul/ **19**/8; **32**/12; **49**/18; **51**/21
storage tank /stórɪj-tæŋk/ **37**/14
store /stɔr/ **15**/20
storm cloud /stórm-klaud/ **27**/2
stove /stov/ **30**/1
straight /stret/ **74**/5b
straight line /strét-láɪn/ **68**/2
straight pin /strét-pɪn/ **53**/12
straw /strɔ/ **51**/12
strawberry /stróbɛri/ **61**/21
stream /strim/ **34**/7
street /strit/ **15**/31
street light /strít-laɪt/ **15**/22
street sign /strít-saɪn/ **14**/7
string /strɪŋ/ **22**/20; **49**/5; **72**/8
string of beads /stríŋ-əv-bídz/ **72**/8
strong /strɔŋ/ **75**/6a
student /stúdənt/ **18**/5
stuffed animal /stáft-ǽnɪməl/ **32**/29
submarine /sábmərin/ **45**/19
subway station /sábwe-stešən/ **14**/3
sugar cane /šúgər-ken/ **63**/9
sugar-bowl /šúgər-bol/ **30**/38
suit /sut/ **11**/6; **13**/5
suit jacket /sút-jækɪt/ **13**/7
suitcase /sút-kes/ **67**/19
sun /sən/ **4**/8; **27**/9
sun-bather /sán-beðər/ **35**/13
sunfish /sán-fɪš/ **58**/15
sunflower /sán-flauər/ **62**/27
supermarket /súpər-markɪt/ **20**
surf /sərf/ **35**/32
swallow /swálo/ **60**/22
swan /swan/ **60**/17
swarm /swɔrm/ **72**/16
swarm of bees /swórm-əv-bíz/ **72**/16
sweater /swétər/ **10**/9, 15; **13**/16
sweep /swip/ **65**/19
swim /swɪm/ **65**/20

swimmer /swímər/ **35**/35
switch /swɪč/ **28**/17; **31**/17; **41**/26
switchboard /swíč-bɔrd/ **21**/15
swordfish /sórd-fɪš/ **58**/3

T-formation /tí-fɔrmešən/ **47**/19
T-shirt /tí-šərt/ **10**/4
table /tébəl/ **30**/26; **46**/21
table-cloth /tébəl-klɔθ/ **51**/31
table tennis /tébəl-tɛnɪs/ **46**
tail /tel/ **44**/13; **56**/23; **57**/2; **58**/7
tail fin /tél-fɪn/ **44**/13

taillight /tél-laɪt/ **38**/4
tank /tæŋk/ **45**/8
tanker /tæŋkər/ **43**/18
tap /tæp/ **51**/20
tape /tep/ **53**/2
tape measure /tép-mežər/ **53**/25
Tasman Sea /tæzmən-sí/ **6**/30
taxi /tæksi/ **14**/4
taxicab /tǽksi-kæb/ **14**/4; **40**/22
taxi driver /tǽksi-draɪvər/ **40**/25
taxi stand /tǽksi-stænd/ **40**/21
tea /ti/ **63**/8
teacher /tíčər/ **18**/1; **55**/11
tea kettle /ti-kɛtəl/ **30**/17
team /tím/ **72**/15
team of players /tím-əv-pléərz/ **72**/15
tear /tɪr/ **65**/21
telegram /téləgræm/ **22**/17
telephone /téləfon/ **21**/2; **28**/18
telephone book /téləfon-buk/ **28**/22
telephone-booth /téləfon-buθ/ **15**/28
television /téləvižən/ **29**/29
temperature /tɛmpəčur/ **70**
temple /tɛmpəl/ **9**/7
tennis /ténɪs/ **48**
tennis ball /ténɪs-bɔl/ **48**/28
tennis court /ténɪs-kɔrt/ **48**/23
tennis racket /ténɪs-rækɪt/ **48**/27
tennis shoe /tɛnɪs-šu/ **10**/13
tent /tɛnt/ **35**/1
tentacle /téntəkəl/ **58**/24
test tube /tést-tub/ **19**/22
text /tɛkst/ **52**/21
theater /θiétər/ **50A**; **50**/8
thermometer /θərmámɪtər/ **70**/12
thermos /θórmɑs/ **67**/9
thick /θɪk/ **75**/15a
thigh /θáɪ/ **8**/33
thimble /θímbəl/ **53**/5
thin /θɪn/ **74**/10b; **75**/15b
third /θərd/ **69**/13
third baseman /θərd-bésmən/ **48**/13
thread /θrɛd/ **25**/10; **53**/8
throat /θrot/ **8**/12
through /θru/ **76**/2
thruway /θrúwe/ **39**/1
thumb /θəm/ **8**/29
ticket /tíkɪt/ **41**/7
ticket office /tíkɪt-ɔfɪs/ **41**/14
tie /táɪ/ **11**/4; **65**/23
ties /tóɪz/ **41**/25
tiger /táɪgər/ **57**/19
tight /táɪt/ **75**/16b
tile /táɪl/ **33**/29
time /táɪm/ **70**
tire /táɪr/ **38**/8; **40**/11
to /tu/ **77**/4
toaster /tóstər/ **30**/18
toboggan /təbágən/ **47**/29
tobogganist /təbágənɪst/ **47**/28
toe /to/ **9**/41
toilet /tóɪlɪt/ **33**/8
toilet-paper /tóɪlɪt-pepər/ **33**/10
tomato /təméto/ **62**/15
tongue /təŋ/ **9**/14; **59**/8
tool /tul/ **25**
tool shed /túl-šed/ **26**/20
tooth /tuθ/ **9**/12
toothbrush /túθ-brəš/ **33**/17
toothpaste /túθ-pest/ **33**/21
top /tap/ **69**/1
torpedo /tɔrpído/ **45**/17
tortoise /tórtəs/ **59**/2
touch /təč/ **65**/22
toward /tórd/ **77**/10
towel /táuəl/ **33**/22; **35**/14
towel rack /táuəl-ræk/ **33**/23
toy /tóɪ/ **32**/19
toybox /tóɪ-baks/ **32**/18
track /træk/ **41**/24
tractor /træktər/ **36**/18
tractor trailer /træktər-trélər/ **39**/11
traffic circle /træfik-sərkəl/ **39**/4
traffic-light /træfík-laɪt/ **14**/6
railer /trélər/ **39**/13, 21
trailer truck /trélər-trʌk/ **39**/11
train /tren/ **41**/1
train station /trén-stešən/ **41**/13
transporter /trænzpɔrtər/ **39**/12

trash bag /træš-bæg/ **67**/3
trash basket /træš-bæskət/ **67**/12
trash can /træš-kæn/ **67**/12
travel /trævəl/ **38–44**
trawler /trɔlər/ **43**/17
tree /tri/ **27**/11; **34**/15
trenchcoat /trénč-kot/ **11**/12
triangle /tráɪæŋgəl/ **68**
trigger /trígər/ **45**/13
tripod /tráɪpad/ **19**/13
trombone /trambón/ **49**/20
Tropic of Cancer /trápɪk-əv-kǽnsər/ **5**/3
Tropic of Capricorn /trápɪk-əv-kǽprɪkɔrn/ **5**/5
trousers /trauzərz/ **11**/17
trowel /tráuəl/ **23**/17
truck /trʌk/ **14**/14; **39**/14
truck driver /trʌ́k-draɪvər/ **54**/12
trumpet /trámpət/ **49**/19
trunk /trʌŋk/ **27**/12; **38**/2; **57**/22; **63**/12; **67**/16
trunks /trʌŋks/ **35**/20
tub /təb/ **33**/1
tube /tub/ **73**/13
tube of toothpaste /túb-əv-túθ-pest/ **73**/13
tulip /túlɪp/ **62**/22
turkey /tórki/ **60**/16
turn /tərn/ **66**/10
turn signal /tórn-sɪgnəl/ **38**/5
turntable /tórn-tebəl/ **29**/19
turtle /tórtəl/ **59**/4
turtleneck sweater /tórtəl nɛk swétər/ **13**/1
tusk /tʌsk/ **57**/23
TV /tí-ví/ **29**/28
twig /twɪg/ **27**/14; **63**/14
type /táɪp/ **66**/21
typewriter /táɪp-raɪtər/ **21**/21
typist /táɪpɪst/ **54**/9

ugly /ágli/ **75**/9b
umbrella /əmbréla/ **11**/24
umpire /ámpaɪər/ **48**/3
uncle /áŋkəl/ **71**/10
under /ándər/ **76**/17
underneath /əndərníθ/ **76**/17
underpass /ándər-pæs/ **39**/3
undershirt /ándər-šərt/ **10**/4
(under)shorts /ándər-šɔrts/ **10**/5
uniform /yúnɪfɔrm/ **16**/3
universe /yúnɪvərs/ **4**
up /əp/ **76**/5
upper arm /ápər-árm/ **8**/22
upstairs /əpstérz/ **28**/14
Urals /yúrəlz/ **7**/39
usher /əšər/ **50**/19

vacuum cleaner /vǽkyum-klinər/ **31**/1
valley /væli/ **34**/6
valve /vælv/ **40**/3; **49**/2
van /væn/ **14**/13; **39**/22
vegetables /véjtəbəlz/ **20**/18; **62**
vein /ven/ **9**/29
verb /vərb/ **64–66**
vest /vɛst/ **11**/5
village /vílɪj/ **34**/11
vine /váɪn/ **61**/13
viola /vióla/ **49**/7
violin /vaɪəlín/ **49**/4
vise /vaɪs/ **24**/8
vulture /vólčər/ **60**/10

waist /west/ **8**/16
waiter /wétər/ **51**/22
waiting room /wétɪŋ-rum/ **41**/18
waitress /wétrəs/ **54**/11
walk /wɔk/ **65**/24
wall /wɔl/ **26**/3; **29**/2
wallet /wálɪt/ **67**/21
walnut /wɔ́lnət/ **61**/27
warehouse /wɛ́ər-haus/ **42**/3
warship /wɔr-šɪp/ **45**/16
wash /wɔš/ **65**/25
wash cloth /wɔ́š-klɔθ/ **33**/19
washer /wɔ́šər/ **25**/12
washing machine /wɔ́šɪŋ-məšín/ **31**/4
wasp /wasp/ **59**/22
wastepaper basket /wés-pepər-bæskɪt/ **21**/13
watch /wač/ **11**/21
watchband /wáč-bænd/ **11**/22

water /wɔ́tər/35/31; **42–43**
waterfall /wɔ́tər-fɔl/34/4
watering-can /wɔ́tərɪŋ-kæn/27/23
waterlily /wɔ́tərlɪli/62/26
wave /wev/35/33; **66**/1
wavy line /wévi-láɪn/68/7
weak /wik/75/6b
weather /wéðər/27
web /wɛb/58/26
webbed foot /wɛ́bd-fút/60/9
weep /wip/64/7
weight /we/19/3
west /wɛst/5/16
wet /wɛt/74/7a
whale /hwel/57/1
wharf /wɔrf/42/5
wheat /hwit/36/14; 63/2
wheel /hwil/40/9
wheelbarrow /hwíl-bæro/23/24; 27/27
whisker /hwískər/56/21
whistle /hwísəl/41/12
wide /wáɪd/75/1b
width /wɪdθ/69/8
wife /wáɪf/71/1

willow /wílo/63/24
wind /wind/66/3
windbreaker /wínd-brekər/35/18
windlass /wídləs/42/16
window /wíndo/26/8
window box /wíndo-baks/26/13
window frame /wíndo-frem/26/9
window pane /wíndo-pen/26/10
windowsill /wíndo-sɪl/26/11
windpipe /wínd-paɪp/9/22
windshield /wín-šild/38/10
windshield wiper /wín-šild-waɪpər/38/11
wine glass /wáɪn-glæs/51/27
wing /wɪŋ/44/11; 60/23
wings /wɪŋz/50/5
winter sports /wíntər-spórts/47
witness /wítnɪs/16/19
witness stand /wítnɪs-stænd/16/18
wolf /wʊlf/57/11
women /wímɪn/12–13
wood /wʊd/34/8
woods /wʊdz/34/8
wool /wʊl/53/19
workbench /wɔ́rk-bɛnč/24/1

worker /wɔ́rkər/23/14
workers /wɔ́rkərz/72/7
workshop /wɔ́rk-šap/24
world /wərld/5–7
worm /wəm/58/21
wrench /rɛnč/24/13
wrestler /rɛ́slər/46/22
wrestling /rɛ́slɪŋ/46
wrist /rɪst/8/25
write /ráɪt/66/2

x-ray /ɛ́ks-re/17/24

Yangtze /yǽŋ-tsí/7/55
yard /yard/27; **80**
Yellow River /yɛ́lo-rívər/7/54
young /yəŋ/75/2a

zebra /zíbrə/57/24
zigzag /zíg-zæg/68/6
zip code /zíp-kod/22/13
zipper /zípər/53/22